Praise for My Storied Life

My Storied Life is much more than a collection of personal tales. It is a collection of vignettes by an ordinary woman from Maine who made her life extraordinary. Phyllis Blackstone writes with a purpose, with an authentic voice that transforms the mundane into something meaningful. Wrap a warm blanket around your shoulders and read this book in a lounge chair outside of your Roadtrek in front of a campfire. Blackstone's tales will amuse you, inspire you, connect you to shared experiences, and challenge you to consider how your life has meaning beyond your own understanding.

Grant T. Smith, PhD, Professor Emeritus of English,
Viterbo University

From the very first page, Phyllis Blackstone seems to invite you to sit next to her on the couch as she shows you old photos and tells you about all the folks in the pictures. From watching for the school bus to charming audiences with her storytelling, she shares insights, meaningful moments, and laughter. A personal and engaging book that will leave you inspired by a life well-lived.

Hope Lewis, MS, CCMHC, performance storyteller,
past chair of Northeast Storytelling,
founder of the Worldwide Virtual Storytelling Guild

I know that when I hear Phyllis Blackstone tell a story, I can expect to react in two very different ways: one minute I will be laughing heartily, while in the next, tears of sadness will be welling up in my eyes. Such is her gift as an observer and communicator of the human condition: its beauty, its humor, its foibles, its sadness. You will find it all here, and more. I highly recommend this book!

Rob Lively, PhD; Dean Emeritus, University of Maine,
Farmington; President, Western Maine Storytelling

Reading *My Storied Life* is like sitting with a witty friend who generously shares how growing up the youngest in a northern Maine family shapes her into the teacher, storyteller and caregiver we get to know and enjoy through her stories, reflections and teachings. This is not a book to be read once and discarded. It should be read and reread, piece by piece, whenever messages of hope, humor, humility or humanity are needed.

Mike Seliger, PhD, Consultant, Executive Committee,
Healing Story Alliance

A breath of fresh air... Having had the pleasure of chuckling at a couple of these stories delivered so captivatingly by Phyllis Blackstone in lieu of the pastor's sermon, I feel doubly lucky they are now in print. Comforting, thought-provoking and wickedly funny in places, the moral of each story is gently teased out against a vivid backdrop of everyday life, from Walmart shopping trips and adventures in the Roadtrek to personal losses and unexpected joys. This is a book brimming with life and wisdom, and one to be shared aloud with friends.

Anne McLintic Smith, MA LLB

The words of Phyllis Blackstone will take you on a journey of memory and affirmation as she stitches your heart and mind together with threads of relationship and understanding. It is always of value to find your own reflection in the lives of others. Phyllis holds the mirror up to reveal familiar images and beneficial resemblances with her stories of commonality and hope, encouragement and wonder. *My Storied Life* is a book to return to again and again to find yourself in Phyllis's storied life.

The Reverend Carla Hubbard Meisterman, pastor of Balmoral Presbyterian Church, Memphis, Tennessee

MY STORIED LIFE

A Maine storyteller shares tales
of her family, travels in her motor home,
experiences in the classroom,
and musings on life.

BY

PHYLLIS A. BLACKSTONE

My Storied Life

Books published by Emerald Lake Books may be ordered through your favorite booksellers or by visiting emeraldlakebooks.com.

Library of Congress Cataloging-in-Publication Data

Names: Blackstone, Phyllis A., 1949- author.

Title: My storied life : a Maine storyteller shares stories of her family, travels in her motor home, experiences in the classroom and musings on life / by Phyllis A. Blackstone.

Description: Sherman, Connecticut : Emerald Lake Books, [2021] | Summary: "Professional storyteller Phyllis Blackstone shares this collection spanning a variety of topics and personal reflections. Committed to telling stories of wisdom and truth, Blackstone's stories evoke universal truths, reflecting participation in a universal experience that encourages further exploration through discussion with others. Storytelling does its best work when it creates a chain reaction. Each story shared is more than the words on the page. They invite further discussion of related experiences. This is how wisdom and truth are attained, and communities are forged"-- Provided by publisher.

Identifiers: LCCN 2021032991 | ISBN 9781945847509 (trade paperback) | ISBN 9781945847516 (epub)

Subjects: LCSH: Blackstone, Phyllis A., 1949- | Women storytellers--Biography. | Maine--Biography. | LCGFT: Autobiographies. | Essays.

Classification: LCC PS3602.L32566 M9 2021 | DDC 814/.6 [B]--dc23

LC record available at https://lccn.loc.gov/2021032991

Dedicated to storytellers everywhere.

Stories of long-ago times,
Stories of now times.
Stories for all folks...
Small or tall.
Stories from the heart...
And good for the soul.
Told with love and laughter for all.

(P. Blackstone, 2017)

Contents

Foreword

Prepare to be entertained as Phyllis Blackstone regales you with the gems she's collected over her fifty years of storytelling. Initially, stories come to her as a thought to be "researched," as she calls it. She gets an idea from some snippet of life she or a friend experiences, and then she dwells on it, mulls it around, plays with it, sounds it out, and determines whether it's storytelling worthy.

Sometimes, she has to embellish it a bit. Not everything about each of these stories is perfectly true. But here's what each of her stories has to have to make it into her vast collection—it must reveal a universal truth so it makes a connection with another human being.

Phyllis believes that the purpose of sharing and telling stories is to make connections. If you hear a story and it resonates with something in your life, then a connection is made and perhaps you arrive at a better understanding of life or of another person.

She and I share a passion for connecting people through stories. As a student of the universal pattern of the hero's/heroine's journey, I collect stories of women's real-life heroine's journeys. Such stories have been told for thousands of years. It's a huge connecting device as the concepts of the hero story are repeated in every culture throughout time. The entire world has always told this kind of story, and we all pass through the same real-life thresholds!

Phyllis's parents were both storytellers. Her mother, she remembers, did a great rendition of the American fable "The Little Red Hen." When Phyllis was a first-grade teacher, she started using her own storytelling ability. She found that those busy and antsy little ones would sit quietly when she began telling them a story—with their full attention focused on her and her words. And later, as an administrator, training teachers, she found teachers reacted to stories the same way as children.

Stories are powerful teaching tools. Tell someone something and they're likely to forget it. Tell them a story and they'll remember it the rest of their lives.

To Phyllis, stories are living things. Like butterflies, she releases them into her audience, hoping that everyone finds what they need in a tale, that the butterflies will alight where they're most needed. By writing them in a book, she hopes they'll reach the people who need to hear them the most.

Whether delivering a story in person or on the page, Phyllis masterfully brings her audience along as she builds to the unexpected climax. We gasp with laughter when we hear what happens—or almost happens!

I have been privileged to hear Phyllis's stories in person and having her there in front of you is an incredible way to experience them—and her. I hope this book will prompt you to reach out to her and invite her to come and tell one of your favorites. I know I could listen to the story about her mother in the wheelchair many more times.

And then there's her story of being the youngest of seven children and having the very important job of letting her siblings know the school bus is approaching. We are delighted when she demonstrates that role for us with gusto. "Bus! Bus!" she yells to the audience. It's perfect. She has set the stage, and we clearly see the five-year-old Phyllis at that window doing her duty.

In a world that strives to be connected through so many technological means, but which seems to break connections at a faster pace than it builds them, isolating us more as we watch our small screens and scroll, Phyllis Blackstone's stories are a great breath of fresh air, an antidote. We read and realize we've had similar moments too. We laugh—or cry—along with her and feel the bond.

Stories unite us, especially stories that hold a universal truth. What a joy it is for me to introduce this book to you. It will leave you with the notion that as long as we can keep telling stories like these, we will be okay. There is hope.

—**Susanna Liller**, life coach, fairy godmother
and author of *You Are a Heroine*

Preface

Born into Storytelling

I was born in January 1949 into a loving farm family in Caribou, Maine, the seventh and final child of Earl and Alice Blackstone. Many of my siblings were much older than me. My oldest sister was eighteen when I was born, just finishing her senior year in high school and preparing to leave for college.

When I was a toddler, whenever my sister came home for a visit, I would ask my mother, "Who is the nice lady who comes to play with me?"

I adored being the baby in this loving family. My entire life, my brothers and sisters were my role models. As an adolescent, I sometimes felt like I had eight parents—two legal parents and six "supervisors." It was hard to veer from the "straight and narrow," so I mostly did what was expected of me.

My mother and father were born storytellers. While my mother read books to me, my favorite time was actually when I got to snuggle in her lap as she told me stories of "The Little Red Hen," "Goldilocks and the Three Bears" and "The Three Little Pigs."

My father was well known in our farming community for his stories. My favorite was the one about how we became a family. It goes like this:

> I was at the University of Maine in Orono studying agronomy when I came home one weekend to attend a grange dance. I saw a beautiful young redhead with blue eyes. I immediately fell into a trance and, when I came to, I had a big farm, a big mortgage, and seven kids!

I became a storyteller in 1970, when I was hired for my first teaching position at the Nash School in Augusta, Maine. As a novice teacher, I didn't always know what to do with antsy first graders. But I discovered that whenever I said, "Once upon a time..." they all sat down. So I learned the value of storytelling early in my career.

In those first years, I only knew a few stories, but the children didn't mind. They kept asking me to repeat them. Sometimes I would make up a story, and if I got stuck, I would ask, "Do you know what happened next?" Then, I used whatever idea they offered to continue the story. Soon, storytelling became my preferred teaching tool.

I started collecting folktales, and over my fifteen years of teaching grades one to seven, I discovered all children love stories.

In 1988, I moved to New Hampshire, and as a literacy specialist responsible for teacher training, I discovered teachers enjoyed learning through stories too.

Later, as a professor of education at universities in Wisconsin and Maine, I found that undergraduate and graduate students also appreciated learning through stories.

By the time I retired in 2014, I was convinced of the power of storytelling and knew I wanted to pursue telling stories for the rest of my life. I believed I would find happiness and contentment through this pursuit. So, one of the two goals I embraced for my retirement years was to expand on my storytelling. (The other was to travel the country in my motor home.)

This book shares my life experiences. But sharing my stories is not the most important goal of this book. The most important goal is to connect with you, the reader, and then to create a chain reaction of connections. I hope my stories will remind you of a story from your life, and you'll share it with listeners, and those listeners will share their stories with other listeners, and so on and so on... until peace comes to the world.

How can anyone hate another human after you hear their story?

Phyllis A. Blackstone
September 30, 2021
Brunswick, Maine

Part 1: Meet My Family

I was born on a potato farm in Caribou, Maine, the youngest of seven children. When I was in second grade, we moved to southern Maine, so I spent my childhood in the Brunswick area. This collection of stories relates the experiences and lessons I learned from being part of a large family.

Aroostook Potato Harvest

My family was up in the early morning darkness during those fall potato harvest days on our farm in Caribou, Maine, in the 1950s. The smells of oatmeal and hot cocoa beckoned us to pull on our old clothes quickly and head to the kitchen. My sister Joyce, a teenager and the sibling in charge of me during the hectic weeks of the harvest, prodded my six-year-old body. "Come on, Phyllis. Get up. We need to have breakfast and get to the fields."

I wanted to stay in the warm, snuggly bed. But, no. Everyone in the family had to help, and even though I was the smallest and youngest of the seven kids, I had to do my share too. A week earlier, we'd gone to the J. J. Newberry Store to get our potato baskets and gloves. I felt pretty important with my own small basket and brand-new gear. I was proud to be a picker this year.

After breakfast, my siblings and I got in the back of the pickup with some of the hired pickers and were driven to the potato field. We were dropped off at different sections. Joyce and I made our way to ours. An empty wooden potato barrel stood at the end of the row. She stuck a square Monopoly-like card securely between the barrel staves. The number on the card showed the barrel had been filled by Joyce (with my help, of course). That night, when Dad sorted through the cards, he would match each card with the picker assigned to that number, and pickers would be paid accordingly.

Joyce and I stood beside the long row of potatoes, gloves on and baskets at the ready. We could hear the tractor pulling the digger. As it rumbled down the row, the digger ground its steel teeth into the soil, under the plants, turning them upside down, unearthing the potatoes, and leaving them on the ground. As soon as the first potatoes appeared, Joyce and I jumped into action. We picked up every one, large, medium or small, tossed them into our baskets, and when they were full, carried them to the barrel. A full basket of potatoes is heavy, so Joyce always had to help me heave it up to the edge of the barrel.

Joyce worked at lightning speed, straddling the basket, keeping it between her legs, bent in what is known as a tabletop position in yoga, picking up as many spuds as she could in each hand, tossing them into the basket, then grabbing the basket and hitching it along as her feet moved down the row. I tried her technique, but my six-year-old body balked, so I resorted to picking on my knees, pushing the basket ahead of me as I advanced along. We always tried to pick the potatoes up in our row before the digger passed by again and unearthed the next one.

My family hired pickers from town or those who came from Canada to work the harvest. We let them live in my grandparents' old house at the edge of the woods. As the pickers filled the barrels throughout the field, my brothers came with a flatbed truck equipped with a hoist. One brother drove, stopping alongside each barrel, while the one in the flatbed threw the circular metal "belt" around the barrel, attached it securely, and pulled a lever. Then the hoist lifted the full barrel of potatoes onto the back of the truck. My brother removed the belt, tilted the barrel on one end, and rolled it, hand over hand, to stand next to the ones they'd already picked up. When the truck was full, my brothers drove it to the potato house and reversed the loading process to put the barrels into storage.

My father sold the farm when I was still young, so I only have scant memories of picking potatoes. About twenty years later, my nephew, Thom Blackstone, who was raised on the same land where our family farm still stood, shared his experiences as a potato picker. By then, the first potato harvesters were in use but not yet perfected, and they led to many accidents. So many farmers still relied on manual labor. My brother may have averted an accident by having my nephew pick potatoes manually, the old-fashioned way.

Today, potato harvest machines are improved, safe and widely used. With so many family farms being merged into corporations in northern Maine, there is no longer a need for so many gloved hands picking manually on the family farm. It has become a story of the past.

What did my six-year-old self learn from that early experience of the potato harvest on the family farm? I learned everyone has to help, and I was proud to do so. I also learned work is hard and I could do hard things.

My Sister's Engagement

When I was born, my sister Barbara was already seventeen years old and looking forward to college. She went to Aroostook State Teacher's College, now known as the University of Maine at Presque Isle (or UMPI). She graduated with a degree in education and landed a position as a second-grade teacher in Brunswick, Maine.

By the time I was five, I had determined that I wanted to be a teacher too, just like Barbara, and just like Barbara, I would wear high heels. Every time Barbara came home to visit, I interrogated her about every aspect of her teaching day. When she was not home, I snuck into her closet, tried out her high heels, and practiced being a teacher with my dolls and teddy bears.

After Barbara had taught for about ten years, she decided she would like to teach overseas. She applied to a program to become a teacher at a missionary school in Pakistan. She was accepted, completed all the paperwork, and had all the shots. I watched as she filled two large barrel-like containers that would be sent by ship with enough provisions for three years. Then the day came when my parents, along with my brother and sister, took her to New York to board the flight to Pakistan. I was going to miss her, and I could tell by the tears in my mother's eyes that she would too.

Once Barbara was settled, she wrote to us often. In the mid-1960s, overseas letters had to be written on special air mail stationary, a thin blue paper, and had to be folded precisely. We loved the days when we found a blue air mail letter in the mailbox.

During the first year and a half, Barbara's letters told us of her school, her students, and what the area was like. However, later in that second year, her letters focused solely on one topic: John. John was so wonderful. John was so kind. John was so thoughtful. John was the nicest man she had ever met. She was smitten by John Anguish, a US Air Force airman from Syracuse, New York, stationed in Pakistan. By the third year, John and Barbara were engaged. They would marry when they returned from Pakistan.

John's tour of duty was finished in March 1967, while Barbara would not come home until later that year. Before reporting to his next base in Corvallis, Oregon, John made a side trip to Brunswick, Maine, to meet his future in-laws.

On Barbara's advice, he went to Senter's Department Store in downtown Brunswick, where our mother worked. Once he found her, he introduced himself. "My name is John. I am going to marry your daughter!"

My mother quipped, "Which one?" (She had five marriageable daughters.) John was invited to have dinner with us and spend the night.

When I arrived home from school, I found busy plans in place to treat John to a Maine lobster feast—the quintessential, celebratory way to entertain folks from away!

It was a feast fit for a king. We had steamed clams, mussels, lobster, salad, hot biscuits and pie for dessert. The four of us—my parents, John and I (all my other siblings were on their own by then)—enjoyed the evening. We shared stories, learned about

John's family, who would soon be connected to ours, sang around the piano as I played, and went to bed with happy hearts.

During the night, I awoke to sounds... disturbing sounds... retching sounds... sounds of regurgitation. I heard my mother's soft voice saying, "Here, take a sip of this tea."

I heard my father's bass voice on the phone, saying, "We would appreciate you coming." Some minutes later, I heard a car on the gravel driveway and my father at the door, saying, "Thank you for coming, Dr. Budd."

I heard Dr. Budd talking to John, finally saying, "I'm going to give you a shot."

I heard John say, "That's a big needle!"

I heard the doctor leave, my parents return to their bedroom, and our home fall into silence once again.

The next morning, when I got ready for school and went into the kitchen, John was sitting at the table, ashen and weak. He was nibbling a piece of dry toast and sipping hot tea. My mother said, "Good morning. We've figured out that John is allergic to shellfish!"

John groaned. It had been a rough night.

I went off to school, my parents went to work, and John drove back to his family home in New York. John and Barbara married, and we always remembered never to serve him any shellfish. In the following years, this story was often told at family reunions. But it was after they had been married about twenty years, when Barbara told us the rest of the story.

On his way back to New York the day after the lobster feast, John stopped at a pay phone and made an international call to Lahore, Pakistan. He got Barbara on the telephone and repeatedly told her how much he loved her, would always love her, wanted to be with her for all of his life, and would stay with her forever *no matter how many times her family tried to kill him*!

Note: Barbara and John shared a wonderful forty-three years of marriage. Barbara passed away in 2013 and John in 2017. They are exploring the universe together.

Mother's Little Helper

When I was between the ages of four and five, my brother Roger was fourteen or fifteen—the perfect age for an older brother to tease his little sister. I adored Roger and believed everything he said. But, of course, I didn't know what teasing was, so I was an easy target.

"*Mom*, Roger said I will never grow up if I keep eating cottage cheese!"

"It's not true, Phyllis. Roger is teasing you."

"*Mom*, Roger says he is going to pull out his ephogus—the thing in his throat."

"It's an esophagus, and he can't pull it out. He's teasing you."

"*Mom*, Roger says I drank water from Ruthie's glass and I got germs and maybe I'll die. Mom, will I wake up dead?"

"No, Phyllis. Don't drink from Ruthie's glass again. But Roger is teasing you."

About a year later, the teasing subsided—probably because Roger became interested in girls. I remember when he announced he was going on a date. I didn't know what a date was, but if he was going on one, I would surely like to go too.

"Roger, can I go on the date with you?"

"No!"

"Why not?"

"Because it's a date!"

"*Mom*, Roger said I couldn't go on his date. Tell him he has to take me with him."

"No, Phyllis. You cannot go on his date with him. This is his time with his friend. Besides, it will be too late—past your bedtime."

That is when I grasped the truth and had to accept it. Mom loved Roger more than she loved me! If she had truly loved me, she would have made Roger take me with him on his date, whatever that was.

As the years passed, Roger had a successful career and beautiful family. I was busy with my career too. But whenever we were together, Roger always teased me. As an adult, I understood the linguistic structure of teasing and could tease him right back. We had a lot of fun together.

On reflection, maybe teenage older brothers can be considered mothers' little helpers. Their teasing educates younger siblings about what is true and what is not. We all have to learn to discern fact from fiction somewhere along the path of life. I learned it from Roger.

The Dirty Story

When I was four, my sister Ruth was seven and going to school. I wished I could go to school too, but "they" all said I was too young. I awaited Ruth's arrival every afternoon so she could tell me everything that had happened that day.

One afternoon, when Ruth and I were playing in the living room, she said, "I heard a dirty story today. Do you want to hear it?"

I pondered. I didn't know what a dirty story was, but I was pretty sure I wasn't supposed to listen to them. You see, I had been a witness to an interaction between my mother and my two teenage brothers. Evidently, my mother heard them share a story between themselves and intervened, hands on her hips, sternly saying, "Boys, that is a dirty story, and I don't want to hear you tell that kind of story again in this house, especially in front of your sisters!"

As a silent observer, I got the message that dirty stories were bad, although I didn't have a clue what a dirty story even was. So that's why I hesitated when Ruth offered to tell me a dirty story. I wasn't sure what I should do.

The situation was resolved when my mother called us to help get the table ready for dinner. Later, there were clean-up chores and family time, then Ruth and I got ready for bed. After my mother tucked us in and kissed us good night, she turned off the light and closed the door.

I immediately sat straight up and said, "Ruthie! Ruthie!"

"What?"

"Tell me the dirty story!"

"Huh?"

"You know, the dirty story you heard at school. What was it?"

It took some prodding, but I persevered, determined to hear a dirty story. I had pondered enough and decided I needed to know for sure what dirty stories were.

"So, what was it? Tell me!"

"Oh," she said as she sat up and looked at me. "Here it is. Two white horses fell into the mud."

"Huh? Two white horses fell into the mud? That's the dirty story?"

"Yes. Don't you get it? Two white horses were clean, then fell into the mud and got all dirty. Get it?"

She lay back down in her bed. I continued sitting up, pondering what she had said.

"So, that is a dirty story. It's about something that is clean, then falls into mud and gets dirty! Hmm..."

I thought more about it. I wondered why my mother didn't like that kind of story.

I mused some more. Finally, my sleepy head wanted to lie down, and I said to myself, "That's my mother. She just doesn't like dirt of any kind!"

The Plaque on the Wall

I remember a dark, wintry day in the mid-1950s in Caribou, Maine. My siblings had returned from school. The older ones were doing their chores in the barn. My sister Ruth and I were playing in the living room. Ruth was about eight, and I was about five.

We heard a knock at the door. My mother answered it, and Ruth and I went to see who it might be. It was a young woman in her winter coat and hat, holding a large cardboard box. She said she was selling wall plaques that she had made. Would my mother like to see them? My mother motioned to the kitchen table, and the woman unwrapped her creations from newspaper and placed them on the table. We thought they were beautiful.

My mother asked how they were made. The woman took embossed paper plates, filled them with plaster of Paris, and once they dried, painted the designs. One depicted a candle with the inscription "Light of the World," and another had a baby lamb in the arms of Jesus with "The Lord is my Shepherd." My favorite had flowers and said, "God Bless Our Home." We oohed and aahed over them. Then, my mother did the most amazing thing. She said we would take one and went to get her pocketbook.

Ruth and I dropped our jaws! She was going to buy one! My mother never bought things like this. We were a farm family. We never had any extra money to spend. We were incredulous that she was going to buy one of these plaques.

When my mother returned, she suggested that Ruth and I choose one. Ruth liked the one with the candle. I liked the one with the flowers. My mother must have liked the one with the candle too because she said we would take that one. That was okay with me. I liked them all.

Mom paid the lady, who wrapped the other plaques to return to the box. Mom, Ruth and I looked fondly at our new purchase. My mother said to me, "You liked the one with the flowers, didn't you?" I nodded, and then the second strange thing happened! My mother said to the lady, "We'll take the one with the flowers too," and she handed more money to the lady.

Now Ruth and I were flabbergasted! We were getting two! We knew our family didn't have enough money for one, let alone two, but we were delighted.

After the lady left, our mother asked us where we should put them. Ruth said the one with the candle should go in our bedroom, and she took it upstairs. When my mother asked me where I thought the other one should go, I pointed to a space on the wall under the clock, between the two kitchen windows. She said that was a good idea, found her hammer and a nail—and that's where it stayed until we moved from that house.

A few years later, we sold the potato farm and my parents, Ruth and I moved to the Brunswick area in southern Maine. My older siblings were all in college or working already. I don't know what happened to the candle plaque, but the flowered plaque always found its place on a kitchen wall, wherever our family lived, whether in Harpswell, Topsham or Brunswick.

In 1974, when I married, my mother gave me that plaque and said it now belonged in my home. It found its place with me in Honolulu, Hawaii; Winslow, Maine; Concord, New Hampshire; La Crosse, Wisconsin; and finally to Brunswick, Maine.

When I was packing up the house in Concord, I removed the plaque and paused to look at it. My mother was in the nursing home by then and had lost her ability to speak. After a long look at the plaque, I asked myself, "Why did she purchase not one, but two, of these? We didn't have money for anything extra. She splurged in purchasing these, which was so out of character for her. She was so thrifty and pinched every penny. Did she buy this because she was tired of always having to say 'no' to nice things for our home? Did she buy a second one because she was tired of her little girls always having to share everything? Or did she buy two because she knew something about the woman selling them? Who was that woman? Did my mother know her? Was the woman in dire need of money?"

I stood in my kitchen for a time, staring at the plaque. I wished I had asked the questions earlier. Now it was too late.

Then it seemed like my mother answered me. In my heart and head, I heard her say, "Phyllis, sometimes you do the extravagant thing because it's the right thing to do!"

The 4-H Alaska Cedar Tree

"I pledge my head to clearer thinking, my heart to greater loyalty, my hands to larger service and my health to better living, for my club, my community and my country." If you have ever belonged to a 4-H club, you can probably recite that pledge too. If you're a 4-Her in the 21st century, you would rephrase the end of the pledge to "for my club, my community, my country and my world."

For those who aren't familiar with it, 4-H is an agricultural club for kids, born out of the grange and cooperative extension services. It originally provided an opportunity for children of farmers and rural families to develop skills necessary for operating a home and farm. Today, it continues to exist and has broadened its opportunities to urban and suburban young people.

I was born into 4-H. As the youngest of seven children, I grew up in the '50s amid 4-H activity. My parents were the club leaders. My six siblings were constantly engaged in 4-H projects, from raising baby beef to canning vegetables, from sewing wearable outfits to baking enough bread, cakes and cookies to feed an army. When I came of age, I too joined the club and began my first experiences with baking, sewing and canning.

As I finished second grade, my five older siblings went off to college and work. My father sold the farm in northern Maine and my parents, my sister Ruth and I moved to southern Maine. For the first few years, we lived on the western side of the Harpswell peninsula. My mother noticed right away there was no 4-H club, so she started one with a neighbor named Edith Marden as her assistant. On meeting days, several of my friends got off the bus with me to attend the Harpswell Red Wing 4-H Club.

In 1958, the big news all over the United States was that Alaska would join the other forty-eight states as part of our nation. It was discussed everywhere, even at our humble club meetings in Harpswell. My parents had the germ of an idea that kept growing in their minds until it sprouted into a project that their small band of school-aged 4-Hers could accomplish.

Their idea was that on Arbor Day (the last Friday in April), our Red Wing 4-H club would plant an Alaska cedar tree on the town commons in Harpswell Center to commemorate the addition of Alaska to the United States. They posed the idea to us, the 4-Hers, and of course, we all excitedly agreed even though most of us had to consult an atlas to discover where Alaska was located!

Then the work began. My parents said we had to get permission from the town selectmen to plant the tree. We asked, "What are selectmen?" When we learned that selectmen are the leaders of the town, we recognized that this wasn't your ordinary group project. It had far-reaching possibilities, affecting more than just our little Red Wing 4-H group. We needed the help of people from every state to create something that would last for many years to come.

The club secretary was commissioned to write a letter on our behalf. Once we had permission, we had to find a way to get a cedar tree from Alaska to Maine. But maybe an Alaska cedar could not grow on the coast of Maine? My father contacted the Maine Secretary of Agriculture, who contacted the University of Maine to test our soil. The results were sent to their counterparts in Alaska, who determined that an Alaska cedar tree could grow in the soil of coastal Maine. Whew!

Now, the cooperative extension service in Alaska had to be contacted about procuring a tree. An Alaska cedar sapling was chosen, packed for shipment by the American agricultural experts in Juneau, and flown to Washington, DC, where Maine's senator, Margaret Chase Smith, met the tree briefly along with the senator from Alaska, Ernest Gruening, who had already been appointed. Then, the sapling continued its journey to the naval air station in Brunswick, Maine.

In the meantime, someone suggested it would be nice to have a bag of soil from each of the other states when the planting took place. The Pine Needle 4-H club in Eddington, Maine, offered to make drawstring bags for each state. Those bags were sent to each state's cooperative extensions, filled with soil, and returned to Virginia Lamb, the regional 4-H director in southern Maine.

Arbor Day would be on April 24 in 1959. We wrote letters of invitation to town officials, legislative representatives, and local, county and state leaders. We were excited to receive responses and realized important people would be coming to our tree planting. The program was planned and printed. Everything was ready!

When Arbor Day finally arrived, it was bright and sunny—and during spring break from school too! My mother, Edith Marden and the officers of the club had been invited by Governor Clauson to his home, the Blaine House, for lunch. As the long-awaited time of 2 p.m. neared, traffic on Route 123 South from Brunswick became congested. I was awed by the long line of cars parked on either side of the road and in the parking lot of the Elijah Kellogg Church.

The program began right on time. Mrs. Hackett, the church organist, played music that could be heard through the open windows. Roberta Weir, a 4-Her who had lived in Alaska, wore her authentic parka and read a poem. After the state 4-H leader and Commissioner of Agriculture gave greetings, Governor Clauson dedicated the tree. We placed a bottle that contained a program and the names of all Red Wing 4-H Club members at the bottom of the hole. The 4-H club president, Brian Marden, officially presented the tree to the town selectmen. Someone placed the sapling in the hole, and the governor was invited to add a shovel full of Maine soil. Then club members from Harpswell-area 4-H clubs and community youngsters came to the microphone in turn, announced the name of the state on their bag, and dumped the soil around the sapling. A tablespoon of soil had even arrived via air mail from Hawaii, the state that would be admitted later that year. So that was added too.

What a day it was! The excitement stayed with our club members for a long time. It was an amazing project completed by an ordinary group of kids with leaders who believed that a small group could do big things. In today's educational lingo, it would be described as a multi-disciplinary project that utilized the diverse intelligences of its members. We all grew up; some moved away, and some remained. But the Alaska cedar tree continues to grow.

One sunny day, you may want to visit the tree. Drive south on Route 123 out of Brunswick, pass the Grange Hall on the left, park in front of the Elijah Kellogg Church, and look to the right. The tree stands with a plaque in front, almost covered by branches, recognizing the Red Wing 4-H Club members who planted it on Arbor Day 1959. It lives to remind us in the 21st century of the 4-H pledge to larger service and better living for a community and a country.

Note: The Harpswell Historical Society holds the Red Wing 4-H club scrapbook containing all the newspaper items, the program and responses from various guests. The historical society welcomes visitors.

ANCESTRY.COM

Many people are discovering their ancestry by sending DNA to online testing sites like Ancestry.com, 23andMe and others. I have contemplated doing the same. But then I remember the story my father always told us.

He told me, and his father told him, and his father told him, that my great-great-grandfather hired a private investigator to research our family tree. He offered a crisp, new $5 bill for payment, a most generous sum at the time.

The investigator went away and did his research. A few months later, he returned and reported the results.

Upon hearing the report, my great-great-grandfather took a crisp, new $10 bill from his wallet and gave it to the investigator, making him promise that he would forget what he had learned and never speak of it to another human, ever!

The Lumberjack's Joke

Note: This story was originally written by my maternal grandfather, William H. Thomas, who lived in the northern Aroostook town of Woodland. He passed away before I was born, so I regret I never knew him. When my mother passed away in 1997, a packet of his writings was found, and my siblings passed them on to me, as the one with the storytelling bug. As storytellers do, I share this story with my modifications.

Before trucks and trains transported logs, the common method was for loggers to float the timber downstream to the various mills awaiting them along the riverbanks.

Several years ago, when lumbering was at its height in Maine and the driving of logs was not handled by corporations as it is now, there was a man named Henry O'Shan who lumbered extensively and drove his timber to the downstate mills. On the river, he crowded his drive as hard as possible to keep it ahead of other drives from competing companies.

His foreman was an energetic hustler named Pete, a small man, but lithe and wiry. When he saw some logs might be headed for a jam, which could delay a drive, Pete would jump onto them. With perfect balance and ease, he kept the timber apart, using a long pole to avoid a jam.

Often, the lumbermen camped on the river's edge, but when they neared the settlements, they hired a room at a tavern or rooming house. They would enjoy a night on a cot or mattress (often unheated), an opportunity for a hot bath, and a hot supper with breakfast the next morning.

It was customary to place favored guests in rooms that were heated from below by a hole through the floor. A rug or table would be placed over the hole in the second-floor room, but the guest could get the benefit of the heat. O'Shan was given one of these heated rooms.

Now, O'Shan and Pete were having a good drive this season. The logs flowed smoothly, the weather cooperated, and both men expected a productive profit. O'Shan, being in a jovial and celebratory mood, invited Pete to share his heated room one night. After a hot bath and delicious supper, they retired to the room, stripped down to their union suits, and relaxed with a jug of "Ol' Be Joyful Fruit Juice"—if you know what I mean. They sat up late, swapping stories and making merry. Naturally, they slept late the next morning, but nonetheless, they were in good spirits.

Pete greeted the morning by regaling O'Shan with more logging stories of his successes and daring feats. O'Shan allowed that, being older, he was not as limber and spry as he had been in his younger years. In fact, O'Shan was getting weary and a bit aggravated at listening to his foreman's prowess. So O'Shan challenged Pete to a contest and even proffered a dollar bill for a bet. The one who could make the longest jump would win the bet.

"Okay," said Pete, puffing up with confidence. They moved the table to one side of the room and prepared to jump from the bedside. O'Shan went first. He flexed and stretched, then made a respectable jump just over the edge of the rug. Pete knew he could do better than that. He limbered up, scooched low and managed a jump all the way to the center of the rug—right over the hole. His scantily clad little body continued right down through the hole and onto the breakfast table below!

The other guests, enjoying breakfast, jumped back and screamed. The waitstaff stopped in their tracks. The cook and the owners rushed in from the kitchen. Pete jumped off the table, dashed out the front door, and went up the back stairs to find O'Shan rolling in laughter.

An angry, red-faced Pete yelled at his boss. "You set me up! You knew that would happen!"

O'Shan insisted he had forgotten about the hole under the rug. Pete gathered his few belongings, grabbed the winning dollar, and left just as the owner of the house barged into the room. O'Shan continued to insist he had forgotten about the hole and would pay for all damages.

Pete and O'Shan worked together for many years. However, neither of them ever spoke of the incident again.

Picnic at Bowdoin Pines

My family loved picnics. My head is full of memories of picnics from an early age to adulthood. They were in the backyard, near the stream at the back of the farm, in picnic areas, on the side of the road, near the ocean, and in a grove of trees.

My mother planned for picnics. She created meals that traveled easily and required little work. My father's idea of a picnic was different. His strategy for organizing a picnic was to grab a paper grocery bag, open the refrigerator, and transfer its contents to the paper bag. The little dish of leftover peas, the remains of a casserole, the almost empty jar of juice, the forgotten apples in the crisper, and the big jar of homemade pickles all made their way into the paper bag. Then, a cursory scan of the counter would produce more items: a half loaf of bread, a day-old muffin, or a few ginger snaps. My father rarely thought about utensils or napkins or cups, so we often ate with fingers and shared the juice bottle.

When my parents, Ruth and I lived in Brunswick, we often went to Bowdoin Pines for a picnic after my mother finished her workday at Senter's Department Store. Ruth and I would be doing our homework after school. Dad would come home, and we would hear him foraging in the kitchen. Then he'd announce, "Come on, girls. We're going to pick Mama up and go on a picnic. It's all packed!" When we got to the picnic tables at Bowdoin Pines, Dad would produce the paper bag, and the contents were always... interesting.

After the picnic, Ruth and I would explore the pine forest, and Mom and Dad would talk about the day. Then it was time to go home, finish our homework, and put another day to bed.

In 2016, after I retired and roamed the country for a place to settle, I found my heart wanted to be back in my hometown of Brunswick. Shortly after moving back, I went to Bowdoin Pines on Bath Road (Route 24). The picnic tables are no longer there, but picturesque trails wind among the pines. I walked the trails, trying to remember where the picnic area had been. I sat on a stump, looked up, and gazed in admiration at those tall pines, which had been growing there for eons.

Then I heard it. It was faint at first, but the voices grew louder. I looked around. I was alone. Who was talking? I gazed upward again and realized the tallest pine trees were having a conversation.

"That's her! Do you see her? I know it's her," said one tree.

"Who? I see her, but who is she?" the other replied.

"She's much older now. Her hair isn't red with pigtails, and her dark-haired sister isn't with her. Her parents aren't here either. But I know it's her!"

"I still don't know who you mean," insisted the other tree.

"You know, the family who came here for picnics. The paper bag picnics. Remember? The picnics that were always a surprise and made the mother and daughters giggle! The girls were very young and played among the trees. The mother and father held hands and talked. And when dusk came, they left. But we knew they would come back again."

"Ah, yes," said the tall pine. "I remember now. We were much younger ourselves. This one is much older now, and she's alone. The others must have transferred to the universe."

"Do you think... do you think she will come back? Do you think she will come sometimes, walk among us, touch our bark, and remember?"

"Yes, I do. See the way she's looking at us right now? She really does love us. She'll be back. That's good."

Note: The Bowdoin Pines were right. I stop by and walk the trails among the pines several times a year and savor the memories.

Only One Life

In late January 2011, my sister-in-law called to tell me that my older brother Vernon had been taken from their home in Caribou, Maine, to Bangor, four hours away, for tests at the Eastern Maine General Hospital. The following day, a Saturday, I journeyed from my home in Farmington, Maine, to visit him.

When I arrived, he was sitting up in a chair and greeted me warmly. Before we settled in for a visit, he said, "Phyllis, when I checked in, the registration folks took my wallet and money. Could you give me a dollar?"

"Sure," I replied, promptly taking a dollar from my purse and handing it to him. He laid it on the tray table.

We had a wonderful visit, and before we knew it, his lunch came. He waited while I scurried down to the cafeteria and returned with my lunch. We had a winter picnic as we enjoyed the views of the frozen Penobscot River from his hospital window. We continued the visit, but by mid-afternoon, I noticed he was getting tired and prepared to leave.

While putting on my coat, I glanced at the dollar bill still on the tray table and asked, "What will you do with the dollar bill?"

He replied, "I'll invest it!"

I chuckled. "Vernon, I know you're quite an investor, but this is a hospital, and it's a Saturday afternoon. Where are the investment opportunities here?"

"Super Bowl," he replied quickly. "My roommate, Charlie, is from Pennsylvania!"

"Oh, I get it! I'll check back later."

I am not a fan of football—in fact, I am ignorant of and uninterested in most team sports. But I do know that the annual Super Bowl game is big and important. Although I didn't always know that. I used to think that the Super Bowl was about having a party where everyone enjoyed soup from an enormous bowl. I have since been better informed.

On that Saturday in February 2011, I even knew who the contenders were, the Pittsburgh Steelers and Green Bay Packers. Vernon was going to place his bet of one dollar on the Packers, while his roommate Charlie would root for the Steelers.

The next day, I heard continuous references to the big game on TV, and by late in the afternoon, I was pretty caught up in the excitement. I wondered how Vernon's investment was faring, so I called him in his hospital room to ask about it.

"Well," he said, "Super Bowl Sunday started pretty early. Charlie and I were both wide-awake by 3:30 a.m. and talked for a while. The night nurse came in and suggested we try to sleep. I hinted maybe we couldn't sleep because we needed a snack, and Charlie nodded in agreement. She brought in some juice boxes and an assortment of crackers and cookies and even joined us for the snack. Conversation turned to the big game, and that's when I made my move. I held up your dollar bill, announced I was betting on the Packers. Charlie followed suit and placed his dollar on the Steelers. We looked at the nurse and she said, 'Okay, I'll go get my dollar!'

"Charlie and I agreed that a $3 purse was not much of a win for either of us, so we decided to start a fundraiser. We would take bets during the day, and all the proceeds, we agreed, would go to the pediatric ward downstairs. But first, we each felt like taking a nap!

"After breakfast, the same nurse came into our room with two urinals. One was decorated in the colors of the Steelers, the other with the Packers' green and gold. All that day, we made our way up and down the corridors, soliciting bets. It being a Sunday, there were many visitors and our urinals were filled. And Phyllis, I want you to know that your brother has more in his urinal than Charlie has in his!"

I chuckled. "I'm so proud of you, Vernon. What can I say?"

Monday morning arrived and the Super Bowl funds were sent down to the pediatric ward. It didn't matter which team won. The guys had fun, entertained others, and raised funds for a good cause. Vernon had his tests and, by Monday evening, we knew he had stage IV pancreatic cancer and would probably never see another Super Bowl game.

On December 28, 2011, I traveled the long road to Caribou, Maine, to attend his celebration of life service. Upon entering the church, I paused at the display table with Vernon's picture on it and looked at the information about the Shriners Hospitals for Children. Vernon was very proud of his membership in the Shriners and requested that the children's hospital should receive any memorial gifts. I picked up the form, completed it, took out my checkbook, and wrote a check. Just as I went to sign it, I glanced at his picture. I smiled at his friendly face. I swear, I heard him say, "Add another zero to that number!"

"Why?" I asked.

"Because it's an investment for good!" That is my brother's legacy.

Guest of the Day

It was late November, the day before Thanksgiving. Snow, sleet and freezing rain pelted southern Maine. I left my home in western Maine in the morning to travel to St. Andre's Home in Biddeford and spend the day with my eldest sister, Earlyne. Visits were difficult in these last months of her life. She could not speak or do anything for herself.

I arrived by lunchtime so I could feed her. As I spooned the puréed meal into her mouth, I looked into her eyes and realized we were swapping love messages.

After lunch, I wheeled her to the living area, parked her wheelchair by the piano, and asked the other guests if it was okay with them if I played the piano for my sister. They smiled and gave their permission.

For the next hour, I played for her. Mostly she just looked at me, but many times I noticed her foot tapping. Music was still inside of her. She had been a violinist and sometimes we had played violin and piano duets in church.

Usually, I played for an hour at most, which was enough for her frail body to want a nap.

I wheeled her back to her room, said my goodbyes, and turned her over to the dedicated healthcare providers who gently took care of her.

I headed north to Freeport, Maine. My plan was to stay there overnight and visit my widowed brother-in-law the next day, Thanksgiving Day, to take him to a local restaurant for Thanksgiving dinner.

He had become much weaker since my sister Barbara had passed away some months ago, and I wondered how long he could live by himself. His breathing was labored, and he had become used to the oxygen tank he had to transport with him. Walking was also difficult.

As I drove from Biddeford to Freeport on that Thanksgiving Eve, the roads were dicey! Several cars were in the ditch, and I was glad for my all-wheel-drive vehicle. It was nerve-racking! I could feel the tension in my neck and shoulders. I hoped the storm would abate by tomorrow and the restaurateur would salt and sand the walkway before we arrived.

For now, though, I focused on reaching the Hilton Garden Inn in Freeport safely, where I would have a hot shower and dinner in the hotel restaurant. But then, the car ahead of me spun out of control, rotating 180 degrees before coming to a stop. I pulled over, shaken up, and realized I was holding my breath. My hands were trembling. I breathed deeply and started crying. I was full of questions, none of which had answers—the only response being, "Because this is how life is sometimes!"

Finally, I saw the Freeport exit ahead of me. I slowed and made my way through the town to the Hilton Garden Inn. I parked the car, grateful I had arrived safely, gathered my overnight bag, and entered the hotel.

No one was at the reception desk, but there was an easel with large words that read:

Welcome
Phyllis Blackstone
Guest of the Day

I stared at it and realized that I was indeed Phyllis Blackstone. The attendant arrived and greeted me, and I introduced myself. He welcomed me again more profusely and announced that I had been chosen as their guest of the day. He handed me a balloon with a gift bag tied to it containing water, snacks, sweets and a dinner voucher.

I proceeded to my room, still stunned. Once inside, I examined the gift bag and its contents. Then, I looked upward and said, "Thank you, God. You delight in surprising your beloved children at times when life is difficult."

The Quilt

The quilt serves as a covering on my bed.
Unlike other coverings,
it remains there year-round.
My mother made the quilt and gifted it to me.
My name and the date, 1973,
embroidered in her handwriting in one corner,
prove the quilt belongs to me.
The quilt is composed of long, rectangular strips
of colorful fabric that tell the story of our family.
The red fabric with green, gold and silver keys
is a remnant of my sister's drawstring bag,
completed for her first-year 4-H sewing project.
The cloth with alternating light and dark aqua lines
and tiny blue and pink flowers
is a reminder of my apron,
completed for my second-year 4-H sewing project.
The white material with black outlines

of dancing ladies became a skirt,
completed for the third-year 4-H sewing project.
The spring-like pastel green and pink swatch
is but one reminder of my mother's house dresses,
of which she had several,
for the 1950s farmer's wife always wore one,
covered by a bib apron when cooking or baking.
Her house dresses absorbed my tears
when I ran to her, hurt or afraid,
hid me when I was too shy to face
the neighbor ladies or the Fuller Brush man.
The green, gold-flowered fabric
and the light blue houndstooth material
provided two dresses
for my high school graduation events.
I run my fingers over the multicolored fabrics.
I don't know where they all came from
or how they came to dwell
in my mother's sewing basket.
Are they remnants of 4-H projects
from my older sisters?
Did my mother use them to make clothes
for her other children?
What memories would come to their minds
as they gazed upon the quilt?
I should have asked.
Why didn't I ask?
Now they are gone, and I cannot ask.
Nevertheless, tonight,
and for all the nights of my life,

I will sleep, comforted
by the touch of my mother's hand
and covered by the tapestry of her love.

Part 2: Occasional Stories

The following stories were inspired by a variety of ordinary life experiences, which have a humorous side and tickle my funny bone. Although all the stories in this part began with a real-life experience, some grew more exaggerated than others.

Upon the Occasion of My Conception

The first smells I can remember are from when I was a preschooler, and the aroma of oatmeal and hot cocoa wafted to me as I awoke. I could hear the voices of my older siblings getting ready for school. My two oldest sisters were already away at college. My brother Vernon and sister Joyce were in high school. Joyce would be ironing a skirt or blouse, and Vernon would be teasing her about looking good for the boys. My mother would be helping my sister Ruth, just three years older than me, get her buttons buttoned, snaps snapped, and zippers zipped.

And where was my brother Roger? He was still in bed! Typical adolescent. He would stay there until the very last moment, and when he heard the call, "Bus is coming!" he would roll out of bed, get into his clothes, grab his lunch and books, and be the first one at the end of the driveway to greet the bus driver, Mr. Wyman.

I didn't go to school yet. They told me I was too young, a decision with which I disagreed. But I did have an important job. I was to sit out of the way by the dining room table. When I saw the big yellow bus lumbering up Blackstone Hill, I would yell, "Bus! Bus! Bus is coming!" At that moment, the early morning scurry became an early morning cyclone. Those words had the power to make my family members move with speed and frenzy. By the time the bus was at the end of the driveway, my siblings had exited the house and silence had descended.

My mother would heave a long sigh. She'd serve me breakfast, then pour herself a cup of coffee and sit at the kitchen table with me. Those were the times when my mother and I had important conversations. We'd talk about things like Groundhog Day or April Fool's Day. Or I might ask why Uncle Edwin had no hair on his head, and did she think he would mind if I touched it sometime, just to see what it was like? We talked until my breakfast was finished, then she proceeded to the day's work and I went off to play.

I was glad when my siblings got home from school. There were always things to do. Everyone had chores, even Ruth and me. My parents were the leaders of our local 4-H club, an organization that provides kids with community, mentors and learning opportunities to create positive change in their lives and communities. So, everyone had 4-H projects.

Life was good. Farming was hard work, but there were great times too, like picnics with homemade ice cream, family reunions, music lessons, church, Sunday school, youth group, 4-H events, and games of tag, hide-and-seek, and kick the can.

Time passed, and we all got older. My siblings left for college and work and, before long, married and had children of their own. When I was ten years old, I was delighted with becoming an aunt for the first time. There would be thirteen more nieces and nephews to welcome. Family reunions became larger, and more memorable events occurred, like graduations, weddings and baby showers.

Eventually, I graduated from college, became a teacher, married, obtained a master's degree, became an administrator, obtained a doctorate, and became a university professor. Then the time came when my siblings and I realized our parents were not what they used to be. Their health was declining, inch by inch.

The day arrived when my father had his first stroke—one of several in the ensuing years. As he lay in the hospital, we noticed something about our mother. While seemingly well physically, she had difficulty remembering how to do simple tasks and sometimes wandered off. In the months and years that followed, each of Dad's strokes left his body more emaciated, although his mind was always sharp and aware. My mother's dementia advanced, although her disposition remained sweet and kind throughout the rest of her days. Finally, we all agreed with their healthcare professionals they needed nursing care. They entered Mount Joseph Nursing Home in Waterville, Maine.

My parents had their own room at the nursing home. That room became our family homestead. When my siblings and I gathered there with them, our pictures on the walls and the door closed, we were home. We had memorable family times together. We made each other laugh. My brother and I played a board game called Upwords with Mom.

As our mother's dementia advanced, she said and did things that, frankly, she would never have let any of us say or do! For example, at the nurse's station one day, she looked up and recited, "Birdy, birdy, in the sky, please don't pee in my eye!" Mom! We were shocked! And there was the Christmas when the church youth group gave my parents a box of rolled cookies—you know, the ones with filling inside. My mother used them as cigarettes. She would sit with a cookie between her fingers, puffing on it as if she was smoking it. As far as I know, my mother had never smoked a cigarette in her entire life!

One day, my husband and I were visiting. My husband was pushing my mother's wheelchair toward the activity room for a musical event, and I was holding my father's arm, walking behind them. As we neared the nurse's station, I noticed a UPS man exit the elevator, hand a package to a nurse, and lean over the counter to converse. As the wheelchair got closer, I watched my mother extend her hand, with her thumb and index finger ready. I knew what was on her mind! She was going to *goose* the UPS guy. Yup, he was going to get a goosing like he'd never experienced before.

My husband was oblivious, completely unaware of what was going down. I tried to speed up, but there was no way my father could move faster. I continued to watch, as if in slow motion. I decided against shouting out, "Watch out! UPS goosing ahead!" There was nothing I could do. How would I explain to my family that, on my watch, our mother got evicted from the nursing home for *goosing* the UPS guy?

Just as the wheelchair got within inches of the UPS derriere, my husband noticed that my mother's hand was extended, her fingers poised to pinch and her body leaning forward. That's when he realized what she had planned and, in a masterful move, veered the wheelchair to the opposite side. The UPS guy was saved.

When my father and I caught up to them, my husband was kneeling by her side, saying, "Mom, I saw what you were going to do!"

My mother smiled and remarked, "It would have been so much fun!"

On a warm spring evening, I was visiting our parents in their room with my two brothers, Vernon and Roger. We had talked about what we were doing and about our families. At one point, my mother surprised us by asking my father, "Earl, which one of our children was conceived in the barn?" My brothers and I looked at each other, eyes opened wide and our faces reddened.

My father sat with his head bowed, his eyes closed, in his best thinking mode, and finally said, "I don't know, Mama. I can't remember."

We couldn't seem to get the conversation on safer ground after that jaw-dropper, so the visit wound to a conclusion. We said our good nights and proceeded to the parking lot.

As we said goodbye, my brother Vernon asked, "So, Phyllis, who was it? Who was conceived in the barn?"

"How would I know?" I answered.

"You know everyone's birthday. Figure it out. Subtract nine months!"

It's true. I am the family member who keeps track of birthdays and important dates. I recited the birthdays, and my brother Roger, the family CPA, crunched the numbers.

Guess what?

It was *me*! I was the one conceived in the barn. I won! I was conceived in the barn! Conceived by two lovers who adored each other for sixty-eight years before they passed away in that nursing home, one month apart. What a blessing to have such a legacy of love!

Upon the Occasion of Being Locked In

One October day in the early 1990s, I awoke to the sun streaming into my Concord, New Hampshire, home. It took me a moment to remember... But then. Ah, yes... It was Friday, and I had the day off! A glorious three-day weekend loomed ahead. My husband and I were taking a road trip to Lake Placid, New York.

We quickly got dressed and picked up our bags, having packed them the night before. With coffee mugs in hand, our car headed west across New Hampshire, then Vermont, and onward to Lake Champlain. Mother Nature treated us to a brilliant day of sunshine that made the leaves glow in shades of red, orange, yellow and magenta. The mountains were spectacular.

We boarded the ferry near Burlington, Vermont, and enjoyed the picturesque journey across Lake Champlain. On the New York side, we continued our journey to Lake Placid. As our journey neared its end in the early afternoon, we looked down from atop a large hill to the beautiful vista of Lake Placid, surrounded by mountains and the lake. This would be a wonderful weekend.

We had a purpose for visiting Lake Placid. It wasn't just a leaf-peeping trip. My husband sang with a barbershop chorus and quartet, and the Northeast District Competition was being held in Lake Placid. His ensemble would be competing with others from across the northeastern states. I went along for the ride and to visit with the other wives.

But as we drove toward our motel, I noticed something that made my heart sing. Throughout the town, on both sides of the street, stood interesting, enticing, attractive shops. I am a shopper. That doesn't mean I am a spender, but I do love to shop.

I live by certain shopping mantras, such as "There's only one more shopping day until tomorrow" and "How will you know if you've found something you didn't know you needed unless you go into every shop?" I can shop for a long time—multiple days, in fact. My shopping friend Jan and I tried to figure out which of us could shop the longest, but every time we tried, the stores all closed before we were finished! So you can understand why my heart was thumping with excitement as we traveled Main Street.

After checking into the motel, my husband said with a concerned look, "Honey, I won't be able to spend time with you this afternoon. The chorus is rehearsing, then the quartet will be getting together. Will you be okay?"

"Sure, I understand," I said with studied calm and an artificial blandness that belied my excited heart. "I'll be fine. I'll catch up with you later at the competition."

As he left for rehearsal, I tied my sneakers, then put my room key in one pocket and my cash and credit card in another. I headed for Main Street, then stopped at the first intersection to plan my strategy. That's right—true shoppers have a strategy. Time must be used wisely, otherwise some stores may be missed. I decided my plan would be to visit each business on the left side of the street, all the way to the end, then to visit those on the right side of the street, all the way back to the motel. After all, I only had *four* hours!

I enacted the plan and enjoyed every shop—clothing shops, jewelry shops, card shops, bookshops, antique shops, candy shops, coffee shops, consignment shops. I am an equal opportunity patron.

The afternoon wore on, and I was in shopping heaven. It was getting late, and I was on the opposite side of the street, near the motel, wandering through an old house converted into an antique shop, when I realized everything around me was quiet. Glancing at my watch, I saw it was already 4:50 p.m. I thought, *Oh, my gosh! It's almost 5:00. I bet this place closes soon. I have to get back and meet the wives for dinner!*

I proceeded to the front of the shop. No one was around, not even a cashier. I reached for the door, but it wouldn't open. Thinking it was sticking, I pulled on it harder, but it still wouldn't open. I tried again, mustering as much strength as possible. It was locked!

I looked around for someone. The lights were on and a coat and lunch container were behind the counter, but no one was around. I jangled a pair of antique cowbells, but that didn't rouse anyone. I said, "Hello, hello. Anyone here?"

Then, I noticed stairs to a second floor. I yelled up the stairs, "Hello, hello!" No one came.

I finally admitted the truth to myself. "I am locked in an antique shop!"

I wondered what to do. After a few moments, I noticed an antique telephone on the counter. Picking up the receiver, I heard a dial tone. (Remember dial tones?) Noticing a list of telephone numbers next to the phone, I called the Lake Placid Police Department.

A male voice answered, "Lake Placid Police."

I said, "Hello, I am a visitor to Lake Placid, and I seem to be locked in an antique shop on Main Street. No one is here, and I can't get out."

A pause ensued. "You're what?" he bellowed.

I repeated myself, thinking I'd been very clear.

Another pause ensued. Then he laughed. I didn't. He asked me more questions about who I was, why I was in Lake Placid, and where on Main Street I was. I replied that I was in an antique shop and, out of the window, I could see a church and a parking lot.

"Okay. I know exactly where you are."

Then, he said what may be one of the dumbest things ever said by a patrolman. "Don't move! Stay right where you are. I will come to get you."

Where does he think I will go? I thought as I hung up the phone and waited.

After a few moments, the telephone rang, and I faced a new dilemma. Should I answer it? I didn't know. I thought and thought. Finally, I decided. *I should answer it. It's probably the police department calling back to see if my story is really true. Police do that, you know. I've seen it on Law and Order.*

So, I answered the phone with a confident "Hello."

I heard a woman's voice. "Er... er... er... uh... uh... Is... is... Greg there?"

"No," I replied. "Greg is not here. I am a visitor in Lake Placid, and I'm locked in an antique shop. I called the Lake Placid police, and they're coming to rescue me."

With another series of ers and uhs, she hung up, and I waited some more.

A few moments later, I was surprised by someone unlocking the front door. "Hi," he said. "Were you afraid?"

"No," I replied, stepping through the door to the porch.

He introduced himself as Greg, the owner. He owned this antique shop and one across the street. Thinking no one was in the store and needing to go to the other shop, he had locked the door.

We chatted for a few moments, then there was an awkward silence. I wondered now what to do about the call to the police. Should I call the police station back?

At that moment, I heard the faint wail of a siren, which grew louder with each passing moment. I looked toward the sound and saw cars move aside to make room for the oncoming blue lights. People stared in wonder.

The police car stopped in front of the antique shop where Greg and I now stood together. A crowd formed. Would one of us be handcuffed and taken away?

Greg explained the situation to the police officer, who asked both of us for our identification. I took out my motel room key, a little cash, and a credit card, and Greg offered his license. The officer retreated to the computer in the police cruiser while Greg and I stood awkwardly, trying to ignore the crowd.

The officer returned and said the story seemed to check out and we could leave. I thanked the officer and Greg, who told me, "Come back tomorrow! I'll give you twenty percent off on anything you purchase."

Taking a quick glance around me, I spied a beautiful Royal Dalton china teapot with tiny tea roses and matching teacups. *Hmm*, I thought. *That would look very nice sitting on my hutch!*

"Sure. See you tomorrow!"

Upon the Occasion of the Missing Shopping Cart

There I was, at the Hannaford supermarket in Farmington, Maine, reaching to the highest shelf for a large canister of prunes, which is a regular purchase for me, when I heard a voice saying, "Hello, Phyllis."

It was Roy from church, who was doing the grocery shopping for his wife, Brenda. We chatted for a bit, then Roy went on his way, and I turned to place my canister of prunes in my cart.

My cart... Where was my cart? It had just been there a moment ago. I turned to the left, to the right; I turned all the way around. It was nowhere in sight!

"Oh," I sighed, "someone took my cart."

Has that ever happened to you? Of course it has. It has happened to all of us. And you know what comes next. The person who took your cart will realize their mistake in a few moments and return it to your aisle.

Sometimes, you are the person who mistakenly takes someone else's cart. When you realize it, you bring it back. And, admit it, when you see someone who looks like they're seeking the cart you took, it's embarrassing! So, you give it a hefty push toward the owner to return it, hoping they won't see you.

I reasoned that my cart would be returned to me momentarily, so I continued through the produce section, picking up items. My armload was getting heavy, and I was missing my cart. I was just about to get a new one and start over when Roy came around the corner.

"Phyllis, is this your cart?"

"Yes, thank you." I said as I unloaded my armload of groceries into it.

"I'm sorry I took your cart. I was in the next aisle when I looked into it and said, 'These are all the wrong things!'" Roy looked around and said, "Where is my cart?"

We both looked up and down the aisle. His cart was nowhere in sight. After a few moments of bewilderment, Roy said, "You go ahead, Phyllis. I'll get another one and start over."

Now I had a problem, a dilemma, a moral dilemma. I had my cart, but my friend did not have his, and I didn't think I should just leave without helping him. As I pondered this, I looked down the length of the meat department and saw a man bent over a frozen food bin with a cart by his side. I don't know if it was intuition or what, but I had a strong feeling that the cart belonged to Roy. So I proceeded boldly toward that man, looked up into his face, and asked, "Excuse me, is this your cart?"

He jumped up and back, raising his hands in surrender. "Er... I'm sorry... I'm sorry... I didn't mean to take your cart! I'm sorry!" He looked contrite and afraid. It is not often that men are afraid of me, but in those instances when I evoke a look of fear from them, I take a moment to savor it. I relish that moment and bathe myself in the power! I confidently secured the cart and returned it to Roy.

Whew! The world was now returned to order. I had my cart. Roy had his cart. And that schmuck down there never did have a cart!

You are probably wondering why I am telling you this story. Perhaps you're thinking I believe Roy should eat more prunes. No, that's not why I am telling you the story.

Perhaps you're thinking we could do a better job monitoring our shopping carts. I believe that is true, and I have a proposal for this problem. This is a solvable problem. Remember when, in the old days, we selected a grocery cart and continued on our way? Now, we take a moment to sanitize the cart with a disposable wipe. I suggest we can do more than that.

Consider selecting a cart equipped with a keypad on the side. The shopper enters their personal identification number into the keypad, which registers that cart to that shopper for the entire shopping experience. If another human gets too close to the cart, warning lights flash and an alarm sounds. And if the interloper touches the cart, a voice-activated warning announces, "Get away from the cart! Get away from the cart!" If the sensor does not sense motion within two seconds, an automated Taser rises from the side, and Tasers the would-be thief the length of the aisle. This proposal would certainly resolve the problem of missing shopping carts!

But this is not why I am sharing this story. I am sharing it because of what Roy said. He had looked into my cart and said, "These are all the wrong things." Yet when I looked into my cart, I thought, *These are all the right things for me.*

I invite you to think of a shopping cart as a metaphor for life. In the days, months and years ahead, my wish for you is that your shopping cart of life will brim with all the things that are just right for you.

Upon the Occasion of Donating Blood

The invitation came as a postcard. There it was, sitting in my mailbox with a beautiful pastoral scene on the front. I turned it over to see it was from the American Red Cross, inviting me to donate platelets. It said that my specific blood type was needed due to a shortage of platelets.

I must admit that my blood is impressive. The Red Cross categorizes it as A positive. I refer to it as A plus! That is not just my opinion either. Once when I finished giving blood and was preparing to leave, the technician held up my donation bag, thumped it a couple of times and said, "Quality product here!"

I decided to accept the invitation to donate platelets and dialed the number on the card. A sultry female voice answered, "Hello. I have been a naughty, naughty girl, if you know what I mean."

I was surprised to hear this statement from the American Red Cross, but quickly realized this young person was in great angst and was reaching out for help. I am a retired education professor and have counseled many young women who think their present problem is bigger than it really is. So I replied, "I'm sorry, honey. I know you feel bad about whatever it is you did, but I'm sure it's not as bad as you think and it will all work out."

There was a strange pause, then the woman seemed to regain her composure and said, "Oh… er… uh… You're a woman… er… uh… I'll get a man."

Before I could figure out what that response was about, a gentleman came on the phone and said in a cheery voice, "Hello, sweet cheeks. What can I do for you today?" I thought that was an odd way for an American Red Cross worker to greet me, but I plowed on. I said I would like to make an appointment and suggested some dates for a three-hour block of time.

"Three hours?" he exclaimed. "You want a three-hour appointment? I don't think I can do a three-hour stretch. The last time I tried, I nearly killed myself! I can't do that anymore. I'm almost forty years old! I have heart disease in my family! No, ma'am, not for me!"

"Oh," I said, "Okay." I was beginning to wonder how intensive the procedure would be.

"But, sweet cheeks," he continued, "I'm gonna hand you over to Ricky. You'll love Ricky. He's in great shape, and he can do three hours with no problem. Just a moment."

Now I was a bit confused, but before I could sort it all out, a youthful male voice came on the line with a rather sultry greeting. "Well, hello there. I understand we could enjoy each other's company for a few hours. That sounds fine. Let me ask you, 'What are you wearing right now?'"

"Well," I said, "it's pretty warm here today, so I'm wearing shorts and a halter top."

"I bet you're pretty steamy and sweaty in that outfit," he remarked.

"No," I continued, "it's warm here, but not too humid. I'm comfortable."

This conversation seemed strange, and I wondered if the Red Cross knew how their telephone receptionists spoke to potential donors. But by now, I was determined and forged ahead.

"I would like to make a three-hour appointment. Tuesday at one o'clock would be fine for me, if that's okay for you."

He agreed it was and spoke about the fun we would have together, but his next statement raised my hackles and sent a flood of anger through me. He said, "I'm looking forward to our time together. I have always enjoyed the company of a fine cougar such as yourself."

A cougar! Did he just call me a cougar? I'm not a cougar! I was so insulted and angry that I instantly hung up the phone.

I paced around for a time, muttering expletives. After a while, I calmed down. I said to myself, "Phyllis, you're missing the whole point. The point is that you donate platelets that can save a lot of lives."

I decided to call again and get over the fact that the receptionists were unskilled and inappropriate. I phoned the number again. This time, a young woman answered by saying, "Hello. How may I help you today?"

I said I would like to confirm an appointment for a donation, and she said, "Thank you. You have made my day. We need your help so much!"

I made the appointment, gave platelets and saved lives, and I invite you to do the same.

Upon the Occasion of the Great Dixie Cup Cover-Up

I went for a mammogram, and they said I should come back because the picture was fuzzy. I went back for more pictures, and they said I should come back for biopsy surgery. I met the surgeon and learned the details of the procedure. A few days later, I went to the pre-admission conference and was happy that the nurse who conducted the pre-admission procedures was my friend Wendy.

"Now, Phyllis," she said, "you will meet many people on the day of the procedure and each one will ask you for your complete name and birth date. That's how we do things around here."

"Good to know." I replied.

Like most folks, I get nervous when confronting medical procedures. And when nervous, I have been known to say some pretty outrageous things. Like the time on a Memorial Day weekend when my gall bladder was creating more pain than I could stand. The emergency room's on-call surgeon offered to take it out. I agreed, and after he explained the procedure and wondered if I had questions, I asked, "Is that what you're going to wear? You look like a janitor."

In this situation, I could imagine myself, after having been asked my name and birth date a dozen times, quipping a smart-ass remark like, "What in hell is wrong with everyone's memory? Write it down. I'm not telling you again!"

On the day of the procedure, I arrived at the Franklin County Community Hospital and was shown to my room. A balloon with Tweety Bird on it was propped against the pillows, a gift-wrapped package and a cheery card were on the bed, and a vase of fresh pansies was on the table. I wondered if this was the usual treatment for day-surgery patients. I looked at the card. It was from my friend Wendy, the pre-admission nurse. Tears came to my eyes, grateful for this kindness. I was nervous and a bit afraid. Wouldn't it be nice if all patients could be greeted with such tokens of kindness?

True to Wendy's prediction, I met several healthcare professionals. The first order of business was to visit the radiologist for more mammograms and a precise pinpointing of the exact location for the biopsy. I was wheeled to the mammography room, where my breast was squished between heavy glass panels, then we waited for the radiologist. After several uncomfortable minutes under glass, he arrived, asking for my name and birth date. Then he asks, "Which breast are we working on today?"

I wanted to scream, "The one that's squished flat as a pancake under this glass!" Fortunately, the nurse attending me did not wait for me to respond. She answered for me.

After much poking, prodding, pondering, talking to himself, and rechecking the screen, he inserted a long needle into a precise location and pronounced me ready for surgery.

Now I had a long, nail-like needle sticking out of my boob! The technicians needed to secure the needle for my trip to the operating room.

One nurse reached into the cupboard and produced a Dixie cup. Yes, a paper Dixie cup, like the ones in your picnic basket or those you use at your backyard barbecues. She put the cup over the needle and secured it with tape. "Don't worry," she said. "You'll be under anesthesia when they rip this tape off and you won't feel a thing!" I was grateful it wasn't duct tape!

As she finished and covered me with blankets, I asked about the Dixie cup. "We can buy surgical covers for this purpose, but they cost fifteen dollars apiece—as if healthcare costs aren't high enough already. So we use Dixie cups. They work just as well."

Now that is an example of Yankee ingenuity! I was so proud to be a Mainer. Franklin Community Healthcare does not skimp on training, education, technology or personnel, but the budget's bottom line is met by Dixie cups instead of expensive surgical covers.

I was wheeled from the room with my Dixie cup atop my boob like a party hat. I'm proud to be a part of the Maine Dixie Cup Cover-Up!

Upon the Occasion of Being Sent to the Psych Ward

Life moves on. On the path from being children growing into adults, our personalities and physical features are shaped. Our emotional and social lives are formed. Each of us is special, one-of-a-kind and interesting with assets and liabilities that influence our daily lives.

I have been fortunate to belong to a loving family, to have a good education, and to take care of myself in adulthood. My liability is depression. It's not an extreme condition, but it is chronic, and I must be vigilant about the triggers that prompt an episode. Fortunately, my skilled counselors have taught me how to care for myself and when to call for help if I feel desperate.

Once, my body was physically sick, and I didn't have the emotional energy to ward off a bout of depression. It was a spring weekend when I spent two days in bed with flu-like symptoms. By late Sunday afternoon, as the day turned into night, I could feel my emotional self slipping, then plummeting, into an imaginary hole. I knew my body could not fend off this condition, and it was time to call someone.

I had been crying for hours, but in a moment of calm, I called my friend Barb. When she answered the phone, my tears flowed again, and I couldn't do anything but pant and sob.

She thought she was getting an obscene phone call and spoke accusingly in her bold way.

I was able to say my name, and her voice softened and she gently coaxed me into telling her what was happening. I asked if she could come get me and take me to the emergency room. She said she would be right over. I picked up my purse with my insurance information and a bath towel to wipe my tears, because I just couldn't stop crying. I only had to wait a few moments until she arrived.

In the emergency room, I recited my symptoms between bouts of sobbing. They accessed my records in the computer system and asked about depression. The skilled medical personnel diagnosed my physical status, and a social worker came in to help me with the symptoms of a depressive episode.

They collected and analyzed the information I shared, and the attending physician came to explain what they had found. He suggested that, since I lived by myself and was so depressed, I be admitted—to the psych ward. I agreed. I didn't want to go home. I wanted to go to bed and cry.

Just as Barb was allowed to come in, the nurse brought in a set of clothes—my ensemble! Barb said she would help me get dressed. There were extra-extra-large pants with an extra-extra-large shirt and the extra-extra-large robe. All cotton with a design of tiny flowers on a faded white background. The ensemble did nothing to make me feel better.

I dressed, and Barb couldn't help but laugh at my ludicrous appearance. I caught a glimpse of myself in the mirror and agreed I looked pitiful. Damn it! I take pride in appearing my best. A line from one of my stories says, "Accessorize and moisturize, that's all we have."

I would not go to the psych ward looking like a slob. So, I tried to make my outfit look neater, and Barb helped. We arranged the shirt in a bit of an off-the-shoulder style. We created attractive cuffs on the pants and robe. It was better, and I was ready.

The nurse took me in the elevator to the sixth floor, where she turned over my bag of personal possessions to the desk nurse, then knocked on the door—which, of course, was locked. This was the psych ward, after all!

The door opened and there she was: I was face-to-face with Nurse Ratched—you know, the stern nurse from *One Flew Over the Cuckoo's Nest*. Her face was serious, somber and far too grim. She escorted me down the long corridor to my room.

We passed doors with signs: PRIVATE, DO NOT OPEN, STAFF ONLY, NO ADMITTANCE. At one particularly massive door, I thought, *Aha! That's where they do the lobotomies!*

Once I was in bed, the nurse asked if I needed anything, and I requested some classical music. I don't know about other folks with depression, but I do know that classical music calms me when I'm depressed. By golly, she disappeared and returned with a battery-operated CD player and classical CDs. It was a fitful night in the over-warm, eerie room, but I played the music non-stop and held on to the musical phrases that have warmed souls and kept them intact for centuries.

In the morning, the nurse insisted I go to the breakfast table. When seated there, I looked at the plate of food: eggs, sausage, buttered toast, fruit. I couldn't fathom putting any of it in my mouth. Another nurse insisted I eat something. I chose one-half of a slice of toast for my eating project. I managed to take small bites and chase them down with sips of coffee.

I looked around the table. My dining companions sat in silence, keeping to themselves. I was glad. I didn't want to talk to anyone. A gentleman across the table watched me for a long time. Finally, he attempted to start a conversation. "You're new here, aren't you?"

"Yes," I replied, "I came last night."

"Are you married?" he continued.

What a jerk, I thought. He deserved a dumb answer. I was about to say, "No, I'm not married. I was married. But now my husband is dead, cut up into pieces, and in my freezer!" Just in time, though, I remembered where I was and decided to keep my wise-ass comment to myself. I stayed quiet.

He made another attempt and suggested that if I wanted to get married, I should try out eHarmony.com. He was on the site and had sixty hits already.

Note to self, I thought. *Never log on to eHarmony!*

The day continued. My counselor arrived, and we had a productive session. The antibiotics were helping my physical condition. When the visiting hour began at 3:00, the nurse informed me I had three visitors, but only one could enter at a time. One was the dean of the School of Education, concerned not just about me but about covering my classes. The other two visitors were dear friends.

I stayed another night. The next afternoon, I called a friend for a ride home. When I got there, a few other friends came with Chinese food for dinner. I was feeling better, physically and emotionally. I was grateful for the skilled professionals who knew what to do to make me well. I was proud of myself for allowing someone to help me. Mostly, I was grateful for my friends, ordinary people who stand by me in all situations, for all time.

Upon the Occasion of Shaking What Your Mama Gave Ya

When I was about thirty, I decided that if I was going to go the distance in my career, I needed to take better care of myself. That meant adopting a healthy lifestyle with exercise, proper diet, and balanced living. I went to my local YMCA in Waterville, Maine, to honor my commitment to exercise.

Looking at the list of programs for adults, I immediately discarded all the team sports. I am not good at team sports or any sport that uses a ball of any shape or size. When I see a ball coming toward me, I tend to squat, cover my head, and close my eyes! That action is rarely appreciated by teammates, which explains my avoidance of teams!

I did notice an activity that aroused my interest: aerobic dancing! If it was aerobic, it had to be good. And I love to dance. I enrolled in the class and arrived early, ready to boogie. It was a great choice. I enjoyed dancing to all kinds of music.

A few years later, when I moved to Concord, New Hampshire, I checked the offerings at the YMCA. Aerobic dancing was not offered, so I signed up for aerobic fitness. It was different but done to music, so I persevered. This class featured various props and followed current fads.

There was the trend called "The Slide," which used a shiny, rectangular mat. Participants wore cloth coverings over their sneakers and slid from one side of the mat to the other. One's inner thighs were sore for a week afterward.

Stretchy bands were another prop, which we used to exercise our arms and legs, nearly wrenching them out of place if not careful.

Then there was "The Step" fad. Using rectangular platforms, we jumped on the steps and did a variety of choreographed patterns, up and down, over and back.

My next move was to La Crosse, Wisconsin, where I discovered my favorite exercise class: Jazzercise. I love jazz! And the routines were easy to follow because the patterns were predictable. For example, if we took four hops to the right, we then did four hops to the left. What was done on one side was done on the other side. And all the patterns seemed to follow a series of four or a multiple of four. I attended Jazzercise classes regularly and made wonderful friends there. By the time I left La Crosse, I was sad to say goodbye to my group of friends, with whom I went for coffee and doughnuts or ice cream after class!

In 2008, I returned to my home state of Maine to teach at the University of Maine at Farmington. I became a member of the fitness center on campus, but to my disappointment, they didn't offer Jazzercise. There was, however, a popular new aerobic dance class known as Zumba, featuring Latin American music. I grew to love it since it was a great workout. However, I couldn't always make out the lyrics—partly because I didn't wear my hearing aids while exercising and partly because the music was so loud. When I mentioned this to some of my undergraduate students, they suggested I probably would not approve of the lyrics anyway.

There was one song I always anticipated. It had great rhythm, but the only words I could make out were "Shake what your mama gave ya." I listened for that line, and every time, I looked toward heaven and said, "I'm shaking it, Mama. I'm doing the best I can. Just shaking!"

I retired in 2014 and found my way back to my hometown of Brunswick, Maine. There, I became a member of the Women's Fitness Center and enjoyed several of their classes. My favorite was non-impact aerobics, which is like all the other exercise programs put together, but in free form.

I especially liked an instructor named Erin. She was pleasant, enthusiastic and encouraging, and had an amazing talent for suggesting images that helped us challenge our bodies. For example, on Halloween, she invited us to think of our bodies as dancing skeletons. My skeleton and I danced enthusiastically for about a half hour, when it said to me, "Why are we doing this?"

"Shut up!" I said. "It's good for us. It's good for the bones. Keep doing it. Don't stop!"

About ten minutes later, my skeleton replied, "Calcium is good for the bones! Ice cream has calcium!"

Recently, there was a class in which my instructor's images and my imagination entwined, resulting in a near disaster. In the middle of the class, the instructor asked us to form a circle, and she demonstrated taking four steps to the right, then four steps to the left. The tempo increased, which was fine. Then she invited us to add arm movements, holding our arms up and out, to the right, then to the left, in time with the feet.

Exercising in a circle with others warrants an extra measure of attentiveness than when doing the same steps in your individual spot. If participants don't move in the same direction, they may easily collide. So, I and the other dozen women in the circle were very careful to keep the same pace, with four steps to the right, then four to the left.

That was when it happened! The instructor introduced one of her images. She told us to "Hold the baby!" When I heard that, I realized we were holding our arms like one would hold a baby, with one hand under the head and the other hand on the baby's bottom. It was a perfect visual. So we continued to move the babies back and forth, from one side of our bodies to the other.

Then, out of nowhere, there seemed to be half a misstep somewhere, and our instructor said, "Don't drop the baby!" That was when my imagination crossed over. I was holding the baby, and I surely did not want to drop it. I kept moving and saying, "Don't drop the baby!" But of course, given our momentum, you knew it would happen—and it did. I dropped the baby.

My hands went flying and my baby fell. *Splat!* Right in the middle of the circle. I tried to recover. My hands got into the baby-holding position again, but I lost count and moved three steps instead of four, nearly colliding with the person on my left. My arms went flying and *splat*—I dropped the baby again, right on top of the baby already in the center.

Then my feet got out of sync, my arms couldn't hold onto the babies, and they went *splat*, *splat*, *splat*, piling up in the center. After that, other dancers started making missteps—their arms were flailing wildly, and their babies were dropping, *splat*, *splat*, *splat* in the center, until there was a mountain of babies in our circle.

The music ended and the instructor strongly suggested we go back to our places. She led us in a series of deep breaths. Slowly, my frenzied breathing returned to normal and the mountain of babies disappeared, one by one. It is dangerous when the imagination takes over the exercise regimen.

I still exercise. It makes me feel good, and I know it's the right thing to do. And, some days, when I'm briskly walking to a tape of Golden Oldies or prancing around my home, dancing like no one is watching, I look to the heavens and say, "Mama, I'm shaking it! I'm shaking what you gave me!"

Upon the Occasion of Being Propositioned on Bourbon Street

On July 29, 2005, I was in New Orleans, Louisiana, exactly one month before Katrina invaded its streets. I'll always be glad I saw the grandeur of New Orleans before the hurricane. I was there to present a paper at a conference. The venue was at one end of Bourbon Street, and on that first night, I looked forward to exploring the historic street.

My destination was Preservation Hall, to hear its famed jazz band. Along the way, I enjoyed live music, found a place for dinner, and sampled my first ever mint julep, which I declared to be very fine indeed.

After the performance at Preservation Hall, Bourbon Street was livelier, noisier, more crowded and alive with activity. I took out my hearing aids to muffle the noise. Then, I heard it. Even without my hearing aids, there was no mistaking it. It was a proposition in the form of a question, and I was not going to let it pass without a response.

I whipped myself around and called out, "What did you say? You! What did you say?"

A young man turned to face me. I watched as his pimpled face grew red and his hazel eyes widened. I could hear him thinking, "Oh, my God. It's my grandmother! I am so screwed! I am so grounded for the rest of my life!"

His look of fear and shame did not deter me. I persevered. "What did you ask me?" I demanded.

"Uh... Uh... I just wondered..."

"Go on," I insisted, keeping my eyes focused on his face. "What were you wondering?"

"Uh... Uh... I just wondered... Are you going to heaven or hell?"

He gulped. Then he inhaled. The pause seemed to give him a burst of confidence. He moved into recitation mode. "The wages of sin is death... and all people who do not repent from their fornications and sins, and fall to their knees, and repeat the sinner's prayer, and change their ways will burn in the fires of hell forever." Then he escaped and melted into the crowd.

I stood there, alone, pondering my fornications.

I smiled. I knew exactly where he was coming from. In my youth, I had participated in organized religion, which promoted such thinking. As I grew older, I rejected the man-made interpretations and conditions of organized religion. I embraced a much simpler faith: a faith that says God is Love and Love is God. A faith that uses the Golden Rule as its mission statement. A faith that challenges me to live like God—for God is Love and Love is God.

Upon the Occasion of a Random Act of Kindness

In late April 2016, I spent a few days in the beautiful area of Mystic, Connecticut, before attending the Connecticut Storytelling Conference and Festival. On a warm, sunny Sunday, I set out to explore historic Mystic.

I thoroughly enjoyed poking around the historic district. At lunchtime, I was enticed by a bistro advertising pizza that had won worldwide awards. How could I resist? I entered, sat down, perused the menu, and ordered a slice of pizza and salad. Then I observed my surroundings.

Across from me, in a booth, sat a mother, father and small son. The parents seemed to be in somewhat of a panic! They were each furiously skipping their fingers across their individual phones. I heard snatches of sentences like "Here's one... a mile away" and "Maybe we can..." or "Should we call..." They were obviously trying to solve a problem as the family pizza sat in the middle of the table.

The little boy, maybe about five years of age, was not concerned with the problem and was eating his slice of pizza. More correctly, I should say he was doing his slice of pizza. He had a precise strategy for doing pizza and executed his plan in a serious manner.

First, he carefully picked up each individual pepperoni, licked both sides with his tongue, then leaned back his head, dropping each pepperoni in his mouth like a mother bird feeding its chick, chewing, savoring and finally swallowing.

Once all the pepperoni was gone, he lifted the edge of the cheese with his finger, carefully pulled it away from the crust, dragged the entire layer of cheese into the air, and dropped it into his mouth.

The next step was to conquer the tomato sauce. For this, he lifted the slice with both hands, brought it to his face, and, extending his tongue as far out of his mouth as possible, licked every bit of sauce from the crust. When finished, he wiped his sauce-ridden face on his sleeve.

Finally, he was left with a wedge of thick bare pizza crust, which he turned around and clamped onto with his teeth. Then he nodded his head, making the triangle-shaped crust flap up and down.

I had been observing this whole procedure as it unfolded. His parents were oblivious because they had greater concerns. But I enjoyed the show, trying to keep my chuckles somewhat silent. When the flapping began, an audible laugh burst out of me and his parents looked up and in my direction, and I smiled at them. Then they looked at their son. Being a conscientious parent who didn't want his son to think this behavior was okay, the dad calmly reached out and took it out of his mouth.

The parents seemed to resolve their problem and remember they were hungry. They quickly devoured their share of the pizza. After a few minutes, the dad spoke to the waitress and handed over a credit card, and she returned it for his signature.

In another few moments, they gathered their belongings and left. I was still chuckling.

I asked the waitress for my bill, and she said it had already been paid. "What? Who paid?" I looked around the near empty restaurant. "The family sitting across from you. They paid the bill for you."

Wow, I thought. *I wish they were still here so I could thank them. That was such a nice thing to do. What a gift—complimentary pizza and entertainment.*

I continued to sit a few minutes longer, marveling at this random act of kindness. *Yes, that's what it was! A random act of kindness. Ah, I know this game. The rule is, or should be, that the recipient of a token kindness must then search for an opportunity to perform another for someone else.*

I left the restaurant, still chuckling at the little boy's antics and on a mission to find an opportunity to perform a kindness.

Upon the Occasion of Receiving Three Gifts

The annual event known as my birthday comes and goes, and I am disappointed that I have never received a gift from you. Yes, you: the reader. Perhaps this year will be different. Perhaps you haven't given me a gift because you're not sure what I would like. Let me suggest some ideas for your consideration.

Jewelry is nice and always appropriate. I am not particular. I love all shiny objects—gold, silver, diamonds and rubies. I love them set in earrings, bracelets, necklaces and brooches. I especially like them in sets, such as earrings and a necklace with a bracelet together. It's so much easier to coordinate one's outfit with a set. I always say, "Accessorize and moisturize, ladies. It's all we have left!"

I also like a well-coordinated ensemble. So many chic boutiques, online and off, are available for the shopper with distinctive taste. Of course, you would be prudent to check the return policy, as I am reluctant to announce my size and you would probably purchase the smallest.

Perhaps gifts of jewelry and clothing are too personal for you. May I suggest a cruise to a warm, sunny climate in the midst of winter? Oh, how glorious a gift that would be!

All right! Enough of this kidding around—and I am kidding. I don't expect you to give me a gift for my birthday. It is enough if you just give me the basic three—the three gifts that can be freely given and received at any time.

You know. The basic three gifts...

You don't know what they are?

The basic three gifts, always free and forever welcomed, are welcoming eyes, a friendly smile, and thoughtful words.

I didn't always know about these gifts. Let me tell you how I learned of them.

It was the summer of 1994, and my husband of twenty years had found a more perfect woman and left me. I was stunned. I was heartbroken. I had a pain that traveled from the bottom of my feet to the top of my head, then sank down to my heart and stayed there for months and months.

So what did I do? I got up every morning and went to work! That is what most people in this situation do. There are responsibilities to be met and a living to be made. I worked, despite the pain, day after day. The days were a roller coaster. My counselor said that eventually the ride would become less wild, and in time, it would slow down enough that I could exit it. Days turned into months. Some were excruciating. Eventually, I found little spots of respite in unexpected moments.

One day, work was especially difficult and by day's end, my emotions were raw. On the way home, I wondered what I could do to help myself. I mentally went through the list of self-care activities I had developed with my counselor. It was the late afternoon, and I realized I was hungry too. *I've got it!* I thought. *Coffee! Freshly brewed coffee and a muffin. Yes, freshly brewed coffee is the answer to all life's problems. I will stop at McDonald's for coffee and a muffin.*

I pulled into the McDonald's parking lot close to my home. As I got out of the car, I could feel tears forming, and I remember thinking, "I hope someone smiles at me. I need a smile. Anyone."

I joined the line and others queued behind me. I tried not to cry. I didn't want to cry in front of people. *Maybe I should just leave*, I thought. But I didn't have the energy and didn't know what to do, so I just stayed in the line. I told myself to focus on something else to avoid crying.

I looked at the cashier behind the counter. She was young, pretty, adorned with neon yellow and pink hair, sparkly rings dangling from various piercings, and a floral tattoo flowing from each wrist up to her shoulders.

I smiled. This McDonald's had a way of hiring interesting young people. One time, I used the drive-through to order the $1.99 coffee and muffin special. The girl charged me $1.42. I invited her to check it again. She checked and said, "Oh, that's wrong. It's $1.24."

Another time, McDonald's had a promotion. If you brought their special mug, you could get a refill for $0.99. Approaching the drive-through window, I handed the cashier my mug, and she filled it and handed it back to me. I said, "How much do I owe you?" She replied, "Oh, nothing. It's free. It's just coffee. We've got plenty of it!" I wanted to say I noticed they had plenty of cheeseburgers and french fries too, but I refrained.

By this time, I was next in line. I had held in the tears. The person in front of me had left, and it was my turn. I stepped up to the counter and looked at the young cashier.

She made eye contact with me with welcoming eyes. She gave me a friendly smile. She asked in a most pleasant and helpful manner, "Hello. What can I do for you today?"

That is when I learned about the three basic gifts that can be freely given and are always appreciated: welcoming eyes, a friendly smile, and thoughtful words.

Part 3: Musings

The following stories, some short, some longer, were born from various real-life experiences. In musing about them, I uncovered kernels of truth and wisdom.

Three Petite Musings

Dandelion Lawn

A successful young couple moved into a beautiful, lavish home in the middle of winter. They enjoyed decorating the interior, and as winter gave way to spring, turned their attention to the lawns and gardens.

One morning, as the wife was admiring the sea of bright yellow dandelions spread across the expansive, green lawn, she heard her husband instruct the gardener to apply poison to destroy them all.

Horrified, the wife exclaimed, "No, you can't destroy the dandelions!"

"But, honey," he argued, "it's a field of weeds!"

"Weeds?" she countered. "Dandelions aren't weeds. They are vegetables!"

In her childhood of poverty, dandelions became a tasty spring delicacy when her mother prepared them with her family recipe. The wife always enjoyed the spring delight.

Perception indeed influences how we look upon the ordinary.

The King and His Page

Once upon a time, there was a good and conscientious king. His daily aggravation was a bothersome page who was constantly yakking at his side.

The father of the page was the king's best friend. On his friend's death bed, the king had promised that the young man would always have a job at the palace, and the king would treat him like a son. But the page was a pest, constantly interrupting the king to tell him something.

One day, the king had an idea. He gave the page the title of Minister of Exterior Affairs and assigned him the task of visiting every hamlet, village and city in the kingdom with the instructions to be friendly with the people and listen to their concerns.

Wanting to please the king, the page did his best to become a good listener. Each night, the page returned and, over dinner, reported to the king all the news and stories of the kingdoms' citizens.

Over time, the king became known throughout the world as a great ruler. Why? Because he listened to the page's stories of all the citizens, considered their needs and concerns, and acted accordingly.

Naked Truth

Note: This is a centuries-old folk tale that has been told far and wide, in various forms. This is my own adaptation of a story that belongs to the ages.

At the beginning of time there was Truth, personified as a naked man, traveling from village to village, calling, "Truth. I am truth. Come hear the truth."

Many people came because they wanted to know the truth, but turned away upon seeing the naked man. Being discouraged and wondering why others would not listen to him, he sought advice from his sister, Story.

Having traveled throughout the world, Story lived in a house with boxes and chests of possessions acquired from her travels. Upon hearing her brother's lament, she had an idea. She outfitted him in a fine suit of clothes and accessories. He thought he looked silly. She begged him to wear the clothes for a week and continue his mission.

Truth did as his sister asked. For the next week, wherever he went, people flocked to hear his messages of truth. At week's end, pleased with the result, he reported to his sister.

She smiled. "Dear brother," she said. "No one likes the naked truth, but everyone will listen when it's dressed up as a story!"

Ode to My Fifth Metatarsal, Left Foot

Hello, fifth metatarsal bone in my left foot.

You are the first, and only, bone I have ever broken in my more than seventy years of life.

On the day I was born, you were there, tiny and fledgling, but ready to accept your role in my skeletal system.

You thrived on my mother's milk, followed by the milk freely given by cows on our Aroostook County farm.

You crept, crawled, toddled, then ran with me throughout childhood. You kept up with my treks across potato fields, then later hopped with me over the granite rocks of the Maine coast.

You maintained my pace throughout life, going to and from work, remaining always with me at play, loving the games of hide-and-seek, flashlight tag, and kick the can, dancing to the Latin rhythms of Zumba, anchoring your nearby muscles during yoga stretches.

You never asked for my attention. Then, on that Tuesday in September, on the historic cobblestones of Old Quebec City, my body went down, and you suffered the consequences of the fall.

You broke. A clean break, a simple break, a break in a good place that wouldn't require surgery. I'm proud of your simplicity in your breakage.

Now I know you. I feel you. I'm elevating you. I'm giving you ice to ease the swelling around you. I'm even consuming ice cream to send you more calcium.

My left-footed slipper, sneaker and sandal sit forlornly in the bedroom. "Why can't we travel on the left foot?" they chime. "What is that bulky, black, hideous shoe-like monstrosity that has taken our place?"

That monstrosity is a godsend. I am grateful for all the broken feet that have gone before me, and all the inventors who said, "I can make something for that broken foot so it will be more comfortable and capable of getting around." It may not be a fashion statement, but when I look at it, I think, *I am fortunate—fortunate enough to be able to buy myself this ugly piece of footwear that my insurance will not cover.*

Now, little FM (fifth metatarsal), I truly appreciate you. I took you for granted. I assumed you would always be up to the job. I already knew about broken hearts, broken promises and almost broken spirits. But I now know about broken bones.

Let me say, little FM on the left foot, I love you. And I love the other twenty-five bones in my left foot... and the twenty-six bones in my right foot... and every bone in my body that has served me in silence for all these years.

I shall never take you or your bony colleagues for granted again!

Love from Phyllis,
The Body Assigned to You

Church Climate Change

I picked up my music folder on that late summer Sunday in the early 1980s and headed to the Winslow Congregational Church to do my job as the organist. The schedule was abbreviated for the summer months—no choir anthems, no special additions to the service, and one generic bulletin for the season.

Upon arriving, I organized my music on the stand in the order it was to be played, from prelude to postlude. This is a fail-safe organizational plan for any organist. The guest minister greeted me while he arranged his material on the pulpit. As he settled into the ornate pulpit chair, I began the prelude.

Easy peasy! Everything was ready. What could go wrong?

Climate change. Climate change is what happened on the podium that morning. That service began with a pleasant climate, then the moods of the minister and organist turned chilly, then icy, then heated, then downright flaming—until the service ended, leaving the parishioners perplexed.

The service had begun with my playing a prelude. As I finished, the minister rose, greeted the congregation, and announced the first hymn. After the hymn, things began going wrong. I waited for the prayer of confession as printed in the service bulletin, but the minister announced the Epistle reading!

What was this? I felt a chilly climate begin to stir.

I started the introduction for the next hymn. He turned toward me, glaring slightly, and announced the Old Testament reading.

The climate became icy.

I waited for the New Testament reading, which is always after the Old Testament reading, right there in the bulletin. He turned again, frowning at me, picked up the hymn book, and turned back to the congregation to announce the next hymn.

The climate began heating up.

I then waited for the intercessory prayer, but he announced that the offering would now be taken. The ushers seemed surprised, but they scurried to the back of the church, quickly picked up the offering plates, and booked it down the aisle.

Oh, no! I panicked. Where's the offertory? My music was out of order. I hastened to find the offertory, which my nervous hands dropped. It floated, sauntering downward. I reached out to catch it but missed, and I needed to play something! I flipped open the hymn book and played the hymn in front of me—The Battle Hymn of the Republic.

The climate was now flaming.

The sermon gave me time to collect myself. I was fuming with annoyance. *What gave him the right to come to our church and change the order of the service without telling me?*

I had to do something. This service was a disaster, absolute chaos. I declared to myself, "This service will be done as soon as the sermon is over. I may not be the minister, but I'm playing an instrument that has a volume pedal!" At the final words of the sermon, I started the last hymn. Everyone stood and sang. The minister gave the benediction, and the service was over.

After he had greeted the parishioners and I had closed the organ, the minister and I picked up our materials and began to leave. We smiled and greeted each other.

I was thinking, *Man, he's getting old. He's losing it!*

Perhaps he was thinking, *Poor girl. She's young but old enough to follow the program!*

As we walked next to each other, I looked down and noticed him holding the bulletin that presents the order of the service. I recognized it right away. He was using the generic one for the year before, not this year. No wonder we were all confused. I was using one bulletin, and he was using another.

I pointed it out, and we compared bulletins. We shook our heads in disbelief and laughed at ourselves. We spent that whole service going through climate change!

The lesson is clear. People need to work together despite the changes in moods and feelings. How will we ever solve the big problems like actual climate change if we're not on the same page!

Manna for You and Me

Sister Georgeanne Doucette passed away on June 26, 2017. Late in the evening of June 25, I received a voicemail message from Sister Clare at the Good Shepherd Convent that Sister Georgeanne was expected to pass during the night. I didn't know Sister Clare. I didn't even know why I received the call. I only knew Sister Georgeanne because she was a friend of a friend of my sister. I can only guess that in the very organized, detail-oriented procedures of this convent, my name most likely appeared next to my aging sister's name, as someone who should be contacted upon death.

Two days later, I found Sister Georgeanne's obituary online. She was eighty-eight years old. She was born in Grand Isle, Maine, the fourteenth of fifteen children. She received a Catholic school education. Upon graduation from high school, she entered the Congregation of the Servants of the Immaculate Heart of Mary, also known as the Good Shepherd Sisters of Quebec. After a lifetime of service as a teacher, she retired to the Good Shepherd Retirement Home in Biddeford, Maine.

I searched through my belongings and found the one possession I received from Sister Georgeanne. It was in a box of cherished letters and important papers that has traveled with me over the years, even surviving the mammoth downsizing I did in 2015. It is a homemade card in the shape of a loaf of bread, beautifully colored, with the words Manna for You inscribed in precise calligraphy. As I held it, I remembered the story of how I received it from her.

The year was 1997. My twenty-plus-year marriage had permanently ended. I was alone, feeling the ache of heartbreak and rejection. Through myriad circumstances, I found myself living in Silver Spring, Maryland, for five months while I tried to figure out what to do next. I spent my days searching and applying for various professional positions around the country, wondering what would become of me.

On Sundays, I attended an early morning chapel service at a UCC congregational church. I felt comfortable in the smaller, more intimate setting of the chapel. The assistant minister, who went by the nickname Joey, conducted the service. I liked her immediately. Her words were so authentic, straight from the heart, and comforting.

Once, Joey spoke about the story in Exodus where God provided daily food in the form of manna for the Israelites as they journeyed to the Promised Land. The manna fell white, like dew, each morning. It had to be gathered quickly lest it melt in the hot sun. Each person was to gather the amount that was enough to feed themselves, but no more. It could not be hoarded or else it would become smelly and wormy.

I wasn't surprised when Joey spoke about manna as a metaphor for daily provisions from God. I had heard this metaphor all my church life. But, at this moment, Joey, who didn't know me, looked directly into my eyes and said, "Whatever you need in your life, right now, today, God will supply it to you."

As tears filled my eyes, I knew God would forever provide for my needs. I was so grateful.

But there's more to the story. I found a friend named Marcia at that church. I confided a little of what was happening in my life, and she took it upon herself to invite me for coffee each week. We had much in common and enjoyed our weekly conversations.

One day, Joey's name came up, and we each spoke of how much we enjoyed knowing her. Marcia said, "Joey is so good. I don't know how long we will have her."

I asked if Joey was moving away.

"No," she said. "Joey has terminal cancer and only has a few more months to live."

As tears welled in my eyes, then in Marcia's, I understood. *Joey said those words for herself too. She is living on God's daily provision of manna for herself.* She delivered that message so authentically because she was living it!

In the ensuing days, I contemplated God's manna for me. God's daily provision of strength and grace arrived new every morning. Day by day, things got better. I received an appointment as a professor at a university in Wisconsin. I moved to the Midwest and created a new life for myself. In a few months, Marcia wrote to tell me of Joey's peaceful death.

But there's more to the story. On a visit back to Maine, I told my sister and her friend Doris about Joey and that chapel message that had reminded me of God's daily provisions. Apparently, Doris relayed the story to her friend, Sister Georgeanne.

Later that year, I received this card from Sister Georgeanne. The handmade loaf of bread shows her creativity. Inside, she wrote this message, which I gladly pass on to you today, as a blessing from God:

> At the dawn of each day, may the Lord God greet you with a fresh sustenance of strength and courage. Lovingly, Sr. Georgeanne

Afraid of Heights

I arrived at the top of Maine's Mount Battie at Camden Hills State Park early in the morning. Ready to settle in with a mug of hot coffee, I sat down on a convenient ledge, looking forward to some quiet time for reflection. Midway through my coffee, I heard a car pulling into the parking lot and car doors opening and closing. I was no longer alone.

Although I couldn't see them, it sounded like a young family. I heard a young boy's voice say, "Look, Mom! There's a tower. Can I go up the tower?"

I heard a father say, "Let's go, buddy. We have to climb the stairs."

The mother said, "When you get up there, I'll take your picture for the Christmas card."

I chuckled to myself about my experiences trying to get the best picture for the annual Christmas card. It's not always the easiest task to accomplish.

I listened for voices from the tower. I'd been there and surmised what would happen. The wall at the top is so high even some adults have to stand on tiptoe to see over it.

Wanting a clearer view myself, I stood and moved behind a tree where I could see the tower better.

Sure enough, in a few moments, I heard the young boy's voice. "Daddy, I can't see. Lift me up so I can see."

The father lifted him up, and then I heard, "Hi, Mommy."

His mother asked them to look at the camera, but in a few moments, the young boy was saying, "Let me down, Daddy. Let me down. I want to get down!" His father continued to hold him for the sake of the camera, but the child became increasingly distressed. "Let me down. I don't like it."

"Why?" said his father. "What's wrong?"

"It's too far down. I'll fall. I don't like it."

Then his father wrapped his arms tightly around his son, and I heard him say, "But I'm holding you. I'm holding you tight. I won't let you fall. I would never let you fall. I love you."

I watched as the boy was comforted by his father's words. He settled into his daddy's arms and allowed himself to be held tight.

I exhaled, realizing that I had been anxiously holding my breath. It reminded me of how God, father and mother of the universe and creator of all, loves us so much we are not in danger if we allow God to hold us.

Ambushed on the Grand Canyon Express

In late November 2013, I received a call from my good friend and traveling companion, Barb, in Wisconsin. She cut right to the chase, updating me on her cancer prognosis. "They say there's nothing more they can do for me, and I should go home and enjoy the months I have remaining. I've had my own personal pity party. Now I would like to see the Grand Canyon before I go. Will you come with me?"

Despite a cyclone of emotions rolling around in my head, I instinctively knew this was the right thing to do, so I agreed. It was good timing from my perspective since I would retire in January 2014, and this was most likely the last trip I could take with my friend.

Miraculously, the details fell into place. A friend at church told me her brother and sister-in-law had an apartment next to their home in Apache Junction, Arizona, and would rent it to us for a month. They did so at the bargain price of $500 for the entire month. We booked it for January 15 through February 15, 2014.

Barb's health continued to fail and by the time of our departure date, she was already in hospice care. By then, she had a full-time hospice nurse named Sheila who, to my relief, would take care of Barb's medical needs during our trip.

The three of us bonded well, and we anticipated leaving the winter weather in Wisconsin for the balmy temperatures of Arizona. We were a party of three, with the emphasis on party!

We arrived at the apartment by evening, and within an hour, the local hospice organization came to make sure Barb had everything she needed. We positioned her hospital bed toward the window so she could enjoy the view of the mountains and be close to the patio, where we spent luscious time in the sun.

Sheila took care of Barb's medications and watched over her like a hawk. I was in charge of food. I would ask Barb what she wanted to eat, then I cooked, filling the air with the aroma of down-home cuisine. I created tantalizing menus and arranged them attractively on the table next to her bed so we could enjoy them together. Often, Barb could only swallow a few bites before she became ill and couldn't eat anymore.

Some days, when Barb felt able, Sheila and I helped her into the rental car and we visited various places in this beautiful desert. A few times, Barb wanted to try her luck at the local casino and was pleased when she came away with extra cash. My favorite times were the visits the three of us had together in the morning, still in our pajamas, enjoying freshly brewed coffee.

Barb had a wacky sense of humor, which I always enjoyed. One evening, Sheila went into town to pick up some medications and a few groceries. After she had left, I noticed Sheila's pack of cigarettes, which had dropped on the floor. I picked it up, showed it to Barb, and noticed a mischievous sparkle invade her eyes. She suggested we hide cigarettes throughout the apartment. Of course, I complied. I took out the cigarettes one by one, and Barb directed me to place them on the window sills, on top of the TV, on the shelves, and in the pockets of Sheila's clothes. We left the empty pack on Sheila's bed.

When Sheila returned, she noticed the empty pack and asked about the cigarettes. Barb quipped, "I don't know anything about them. I've been in this bed all evening."

Sheila turned to me, and because I'm a lousy liar, my face reddened and I pointed to Barb. "She's a terrible influence!"

The three of us chuckled throughout the evening every time Sheila found another cigarette.

The main purpose of this trip was to get Barb to the Grand Canyon. It required an overnight stay, and it took some time to work out the details. In the meantime, Sheila and I noticed Barb was growing weaker. We decided to drive to Williams, stay overnight, take the day-long train excursion to the Grand Canyon, return to Williams to stay a second night, then drive back to the apartment.

The plan worked well. The train staff made all arrangements, and a van was waiting for us at the train station. The day was a little cold, but the sun shone brightly. Barb loved trains and was delighted with the excursion. The opportunity to see the Grand Canyon was a bonus. Everything went well. At the rim of the Grand Canyon, we surveyed the beauty of the expanse, held hands, and cried. It was a memorable moment.

Barb was pretty fatigued by the time of the return train trip in the afternoon. In fact, all three of us nodded off in the warmth of the afternoon sun. Then, the train stopped abruptly.

A posse of masked actors in cowboy costumes leapt on the train, passing through the cars, enacting a good old-fashioned ambush. The invaders had toy pistols and playfully demanded that passengers surrender their prized possessions. "This is a hold-up! Put any valuables in this bag! Do what you're told, and no one gets hurt!"

We watched this drama as the troupe made their way to our part of the train. When they got to Barb's seat, she didn't say anything but held up our hotel room key in their faces and smiled! The bandits were speechless... looked at each other... and took a moment to get into the spirit of Barb's silent invitation. Their improvisational skills took over, and my, did they have fun! Everyone in that train car was laughing and hooting all the way to the station.

Our party of three arrived back in Wisconsin, full of love for each other and the memories we had made. Barb passed away ten days later. Whenever I think of her now, I automatically smile and enjoy remembering one of our escapades.

Thank you, Barb, for bringing so much laughter to our friendship!

Give Us Your Hungry, Your Poor

"Food insecurity." That's what we call it now. I don't know how that term got started, but it seems to be the official term. It refers to people who are hungry, including those who may not have enough food at this moment or may not have enough food for later today, tomorrow, next week or next month.

Have you ever been walking along the streets in a city and had people approach you for money to get food? I am always puzzled by what to do.

Because I am a storyteller, I tend to be curious about the people who ask for my help. I wonder what circumstances led them to hunger.

I learned some valuable lessons from my own experiences. Here are just a few.

. . • . .

It was late in the afternoon on a warm spring Sunday in Toronto, Ontario. I was at a professional conference for a few days, and I had all day Sunday to explore before leaving on Monday morning.

The gloriously sunny day beckoned me toward the waterfront, where I joined others enjoying the sunshine. The day passed all too quickly, and it was late afternoon when I headed back to the hotel to prepare for an early morning flight.

I stopped at a little store and, with my remaining cash, stocked up on snacks for the plane ride home. Upon exiting the store, a lady approached me. She was an older woman, stooped over, with messy gray hair and deep facial lines. She asked for money for food. I truly did not have any cash. My plan was to hit the hotel ATM for cash for the trip home. I offered her some of the food from my bag—an apple, an orange, a granola bar, some crispy crackers.

She smiled as I pulled them out of the bag, but declined each one. I wondered why she was refusing my offerings. After all, isn't something better than nothing?

Finally, she opened her mouth wide and pointed. She only had a couple of teeth, and the places where other teeth used to be were red and swollen. There was no way she could eat any of the items I'd offered her.

Folks living with food insecurity often face more than one challenge.

. . • . .

A couple of years later, on an equally warm spring day in St. Louis, Missouri, I was visiting the iconic Gateway Arch and enjoying a nearby park. I was walking along the river when a young woman approached me. She was gaunt, dressed in shabby clothes, and looked forlorn. I knew she was going to ask me for money, and I also knew I was going to give her the few bills in my pocket.

When she asked me for money for food, I asked her where she would go for food if she had money. She mentioned a café further up the street, where she would get some hot soup and bread.

Just then, I noticed out of the corner of my eye some diners coming out of a restaurant across the street. One woman carried a doggie bag and looked our way. She pressed the bag into the hands of a young girl, presumably her daughter, and pointed to us. The girl crossed the street and handed the package to the woman I was talking with, then disappeared back to her family.

The woman opened the bag, took out a Styrofoam box, opened it and asked, "What is this?"

I saw the remains of a Blooming Onion. A Blooming Onion begins with a huge onion, which is cut into wedges, separated, heavily breaded and deep-fried. It is usually served as an appetizer with a dipping sauce and is meant to be shared. A health professional would call it a "heart attack on a plate," but it is tasty when hot from the fryer!

I looked at the now mangled, cold appetizer. It was a slimy, congealed mess! I would not want to reach into the container for a sample, knowing all the human germs that now resided there. I saw by the woman's face that she found it disgusting too.

We walked to the end of the street. She pointed to the café she had mentioned earlier, and I gave her the money from my pocket, telling her, "I hope they have your favorite soup today." She thanked me, and I watched her walk away, still clutching the Styrofoam box.

As I walked, I was bothered. Why, oh why, do we humans think we are doing so much good when we give our leftover messes to the most vulnerable? We do it with leftover food and other items too. I know of parents who think it is so charitable to ask their children to give their toys to poor children so there will be room for new toys in their toy box. The message to the children is that they are worthy of new toys, but poor children can make do with used and tattered ones. Why do we think we have done such a good deed when we haven't treated people the way we'd like to be treated ourselves?

. . • . .

When I taught at Viterbo University, a Franciscan liberal arts university in La Crosse, Wisconsin, I soon learned about the Place of Grace. Two religious studies professors had purchased an old house in the poorest part of town and created a place for hot meals, assistance and community.

I was searching for a place for my fledgling storytelling guild to do a storytelling program and was pleased when Earl Madary, one of the founding professors, welcomed a program after dinner one evening. He knew that most Place of Grace patrons did not have opportunities to attend live performances of any kind.

Our storytelling group gathered early on the scheduled evening to help serve. Earl gave us instructions as we took our positions on the serving line. He said, "For every person who comes through this line, you think of that person as the most honored and important guest to ever come to your home. You greet them with friendliness. You offer more. You do whatever you can to make this person feel loved."

I took that message to heart and know for certain that Jesus would offer the same instructions. In my experiences since then, I have had several opportunities to serve meals to hungry people, and I have always tried to follow Earl's instructions.

Since retiring to my hometown of Brunswick, Maine, I have had the opportunity to practice the principles of the Place of Grace. I learned about these principles at the Neighborhood Café in Bath, Maine, a project of the congregational church that provides a weekly meal for the community. All are welcome. Volunteers arrive early to create tempting, nutritious meals. Others place tablecloths, flowers and silverware on the round tables. I arrive in the late afternoon with my apron, ready to serve meals, bus tables, fetch items, and help in whatever way I can.

A while ago, the minister asked if I would lead the prayer before the meal started. I put strips of paper and pencils on the tables and asked people to write what they were thankful for when they came to the café. I collected the papers and as I read each one, I asked the diners to respond with "Thank You, God." Later, as I reviewed the responses, sorting them into categories, I saw one-third of the papers mentioned the good food, but two-thirds of them indicated they were most grateful for the people, for friends, and for the time to spend together.

As the serving ended and the clean-up began, folks pulled out the take-home containers they were invited to bring, and we filled them with leftovers. People left with their hunger satisfied, a good feeling from being with friends, and a container of food security in their hands.

Slaying the Monsters

Note: The following story was created for a Lenten presentation that focused on the question, "In a world of so much brokenness, how do we claim space for hope and love?" The circumstances of the four young characters illustrate brokenness. Discussion of their diverse issues can be used to find space for hope.

Richard

"Hurry up, Tommy!" yelled twelve-year-old Richard. He wanted to get home quickly. It was Monday, and that meant their mother would just be pulling a batch of chocolate chip cookies out of the oven. Monday was her day off, and for as long as he could remember, this was the day she'd make their favorite cookies. He could hardly wait to bite into that warm, sweet, chocolaty treat.

"Come on, Tommy. Hurry up!" Richard sighed. His little brother was so slow. He was six, and it was Richard's job to walk him home every afternoon. He helped Tommy put his backpack on and grabbed his hand, and they headed out the school door. Sometimes, they could even smell the cookies while still down the street.

"I'll race ya, Tommy." The boys took off, running up the driveway and into the house. "Mom, we're home!" they announced as they flung their backpacks on the table. "Mom, Mom!"

The boys ran through the house. Where was Mom? They looked upstairs and in the backyard. Mom wasn't there! Where could she be?

Richard looked for a note. No note. Something must have happened. What was going on?

Richard looked at his brother. Tommy's eyes were filling with tears. "It will be all right, Tommy. Mom must have had to go somewhere. She'll be back."

Jennie

Fifteen-year-old Jennie squinted at the clock again. 7:03. Three more hours until the mall opened. She sat up in bed and emptied the cash from her purse onto the nightstand. She knew exactly how much money she had, but counted it again. It had taken her almost a year to save this much—mostly from babysitting. *I sure chased around a lot of little brats for this money*, she thought.

She heard noises in the kitchen. "Oh, good. Mom is up." They were going to the mall today, and Jennie would head straight to the sports shop where, for over a year now, she had been trying on the most beautiful jacket. It was black with satin sleeves, gray leather patches, a cotton collar, and an LA Raiders logo printed boldly on the back. Her mother had allowed her to put it on layaway. While it had taken a long time to save the money, she knew it would be worth the wait. She could just see the looks on her friends' faces when they saw her jacket. She would be the envy of everyone.

At 9:35 a.m., Jennie couldn't wait any longer. "Let's go, Mom. The mall will be open by the time we get there."

Her mom chuckled. "Okay, just one more sip of coffee, and I'll get my coat."

Jennie wasn't going to wear a coat herself, but her mother insisted. "Okay, but I'll never have to wear this raggedy, old thing again."

It was a cool December day. The snowflakes were gently falling, and the sun was shining at the same time. When they got to the mall, they agreed to meet in forty-five minutes, and Jennie headed directly to the upscale sports store. Today, the jacket would be hers.

After she paid for it, she slipped her arms into the smooth fleece lining. It fit just right. She asked the salesperson to take off the tags. Then she left the store and headed out onto the street to see how her new jacket felt in the cool outside air.

John

John was already mad. This wasn't shaping up to be a good day. All he wanted was a shower! He just wanted to look halfway decent for school. But when he turned on the squeaky faucet, a thick, smelly substance dribbled out. "Damn."

He got dressed and turned on the faucet in the sink to brush his teeth. The same smelly brown substance oozed out. "Damn!"

From downstairs, in the project where he lived, he could hear his dad—drunk again. Leaving the bathroom, he saw his mother and the terrified look on her face. His dad often hit them when he was drunk.

Suddenly, his dad barreled to the top of the stairs, grabbed her and was about to hit her when John yelled, "Leave her alone, old man!" Then, his dad turned his rage toward John. Before he had time to duck, his dad socked him hard in the right eye. The pain and swelling started immediately.

Furious with his father and frustrated by his own pathetic life, John ran out of the house. When he got to the corner, he saw the taillights of the school bus a block away. He started running, but then slowed to a walk. He knew he would be late again, without an excuse, but at least he could take a shower after gym class and have lunch.

As he walked by the bar and pool hall, a group of know-nothing dropouts taunted him. "What happened to you, jerk-face? Did someone kick your ass?"

John glared at them and kept on walking. *The whole world is mean!* he thought.

And inevitably, as if to prove him right, the principal was at the front entrance when he got to school.

"John, you're tardy again! In fact, I checked. This is the seventh time this month! Be in my office right after school. I'm calling your parents."

Then the principal noticed John's face. "I see you've been fighting again, John. That's another thing I'll let your parents know. I hope you weren't fighting on school property. If you were, you're in big trouble, young man!"

When he got to the classroom, he was met by an elderly looking substitute teacher, glaring at him, and demanding a tardy slip. Since he didn't have one, she yelled at him to go to the office to get one.

Tamika

Tamika sat in her fourth-grade classroom chewing on her pencil. Her mind was buzzing with ideas. She was staring at an empty sheet of lined paper, trying to think of a way to begin the poem the teacher had assigned. You had to think of a person or people you knew and write about them in one of the several types of poems they had studied.

"Poetry flows from the soul and onto the paper," her teacher had said.

Well, Tamika was ready for her poem to flow.

Richard

It had been nearly forty-five minutes and still no Mom. Richard wondered what he was going to do. Tommy just sat, sobbing.

"It's okay, Tommy. Don't cry."

Just then, the lady from next door came over and said, "Come on. I just heard from your dad. I will take you to the hospital!"

They piled into her car and drove off. She stopped in front of an enormous door that said EMERGENCY.

Their neighbor rushed through the door and told the lady at the desk their names. The nurse rushed toward them and said, "Come with me." Tommy started crying again, so Richard took his hand.

The lady led them through a door into a smaller room, where people in masks were rushing around. Richard saw they were all focused on something on a table. Then he saw a face. It was his mother, with tubes coming out of her mouth and nose and arms.

Richard looked away. In a corner of the room, he saw a man bent over and crying hard. It was his dad. But his dad didn't notice them until Tommy let go of Richard's hand and ran to him. His dad stood, picked up Tommy, and embraced Richard.

"What happened, Dad? What happened to Mom?" Richard was having trouble speaking. His words got choked up in his throat.

His dad said something terrible had happened. A crazy, drunk man came into the house and started shooting. The police thought the man was in the wrong house. That was all Dad could say before he started crying again. The three of them huddled in the corner, hanging on to each other while the people in white gowns and masks rushed around.

After a time, the nurses left and his dad brought them to the bed. Richard could see his mother's eyes were closed. He looked at all the tubes and the machines making noises next to the bed. When he looked back at her, her eyes were open. She looked intensely at him. She tried to smile, but he could tell she was in a lot of pain.

"Richard... Richard, I love you." Her voice was weak and raspy. "I love you. Take care of your little brother."

She looked at his dad and then at Tommy and said, "I love you. I love you all so much." After which, she closed her eyes.

Richard wished she would open them again and say something else. But she didn't. He heard his father gasp and start to cry.

A nurse came in and checked the monitors. She said Mom was gone.

Tommy asked, "Where? Where did she go?"

But Richard knew. Mom was dead.

Their dad gently guided them out of the room.

Jennie

It was a great day to be newly tarred pavement. The lazy snowflakes fell on the asphalt, where the warm sun melted them immediately. It was getting a gentle bath when it felt the light dance of a 15-year-old wearing a new jacket. It could feel the excitement in the light steps of this happy creature.

Suddenly, an awful sound invaded the space—the screech of car tires burning rubber into the asphalt's surface. The car slammed to a stop. Footsteps thumped on the pavement. Male voices shouted.

"Give us that jacket, bitch!" they screamed, as three bullies ganged up on the light-footed dancer.

"No, it's mine," cried the girl. "Stop!"

But the gang pushed her down. As they pulled off the jacket and grabbed her purse, the asphalt felt the smooth skin of the young girl scraping across its coarse surface. Feeling new liquid—water from tears and warm blood—the asphalt heard a bone-crushing crack.

The bullies jumped back into the car with their stolen goods and sped off, while the solid asphalt held her body—her sobbing, bruised body.

John

John looked at the old biddy of a substitute teacher. The collected rage of the morning clotted in the pit of his stomach. Something snapped in his brain. "You know what? You've had enough. Enough of people hitting you; enough of people grabbing and yelling. Enough of people blaming you. Enough of putting up with the meanness all around you!"

John heard the old biddy's command to get to the office. "Make me, you bitch!" he yelled into her face.

She grabbed him by the shirt and tried to force him out the door.

But John would not let one more person be mean to him today. He shoved his fist into the old lady's chest. She was knocked backward, lost her balance, and fell to the floor. John started kicking chairs and desks and knocked a stack of books to the ground. Then everything was quiet.

For the first time, John noticed his classmates all staring at him with fear on their faces. One person jumped up and ran out the door.

John looked around. Had he done this? He crumpled to the floor and quietly sobbed.

Tamika

Tamika's thoughts drifted to her neighborhood. Richard and Tommy's mother was shot by a crazy man with a gun. Her babysitter, Jennie, was mugged by mean boys who took her new jacket and purse. They pushed her down on the pavement, and she broke her foot. The man upstairs got drunk and hit people. He hit his wife and his son John and was very mean.

After a bit, the poetry in Tamika's soul flowed. Words spilled onto the paper. She kept thinking of new words to write. She read them over. Sometimes, she erased words. Other times, she changed or added words until they sounded just right in her head. Finally, it was ready. Soon, she would read it to the class. She rehearsed it silently.

When it was her turn, Tamika stood tall and straight before the class—just like the teacher had instructed. She spoke in a clear, strong voice.

Guns are bad.
They make me sad.
They kill people.
That makes me mad.
Mean people don't sing,
They just do mean things.
They rob and steal whatever they want,
In fall, winter, summer and spring.
Some people hit
When they're having a fit.
They give people bruises and black eyes.
They should be put in a pit.
Hate is a monster we all need to slay,
If we don't, we won't be able to play.
Let's have no more meanness or badness,
Let's be nice, so the neighborhood is a good place to stay.

Shh... Hush

Shh... the mother crooned to her whimpering child.
Hush, my baby. Don't you cry.
I'll stay right here and sing you a lullaby.

Shh... said the father to his toddler child.
Hush, my little one. Don't you cry.
I'll bandage your owie, then we'll have pie.

Shh... the teacher instructed her students huddled in the closet.
Hush, my pupils. Don't you cry.
The man with the gun will leave by and by.

Shh... the counselor assured the teenage addict.
Hush, my young one. Don't you cry.
The doctor's shot will bring you down from the high.

Shh... said one neighbor to the other.
Hush, my friend. Don't you cry.
The flood will recede, and we'll be dry.

Shh... said the boss to his workers.
Hush, my comrades. Don't you cry.
The wild fire will be doused, and we won't fry.

Shh... said the doctor to his patient.
Hush, Patient #526. Don't you cry.
You have COVID, but I'll try not to let you die.

Shh... said the husband to his frightened wife.
Hush, my darling. Don't you cry.
The SWAT team is coming, and the hostages will fly.

Shh... said one hostage to another,
Hush, my coworker. Don't you cry.
We'll stay hidden together and quietly on this floor lie.

Shh... said the senator to her colleague,
Hush, my fellow American. Don't you cry.
The National Guard has been called and help is nigh.

Shh... my outer self said to my inner self,
Hush, my ordinary person. Don't you cry.
All will be well with help from On High.

One Time

One time as a child... I found a large chocolate bunny in my Easter basket and ate the whole thing before breakfast! My tummy didn't feel so good, and I had no more chocolate left, only a handful of assorted jelly beans and those marshmallow-filled eggs I dislike. I learned about moderation and not to be selfish—to others or to myself.

One time as a novice teacher... I started to show a movie to my young students, only to discover that it was a porn movie with the same title I meant to show. I learned that teacher preparation requires thoroughness, such as previewing a movie.

One time my father passed away... and in thirty days' time, my mother followed. I learned what it means to be an orphan.

One time my husband told me... he had found someone else to share his life. I learned about plodding through pain and creating a new story.

One time my brother passed away... and five more times, my four sisters and another brother followed. I learned, indeed, am still learning, how to be an elder in my family.

The "one times" compose the structure of my life, and perhaps your life too. When the "one times" of my life intersect with the "one times" of your life, I learn what it means to be blessed.

Alice Mae Has a Party

Alice Mae was an old lady now at ninety-five years old. She lived by herself in a little apartment in a retirement community. Her parents had passed away many years before. She was an only child and had no living relatives, but she had many friends... friends from all over the world. She loved reading and writing and keeping in touch with her friends on the computer.

Now it was Christmas Eve. After dinner, she poured a glass of her favorite wine, and she raised it to make a toast. Her mind returned to her favorite memory of all.

When Alice Mae was six years old and in first grade, she loved everything about her school. She adored her friends and teacher. She enjoyed carrying her lunch in her own lunch bag. Reading and numbers and all the projects the class did together were fun for her. But, at the end of November, her parents said they would be moving for Daddy's job. They would be buying a new house and living in a different town, and Alice Mae would go to a new school.

"No!" said Alice Mae. "I don't want to move! I like it here. I like my school. I don't want to leave my friends!"

Her parents were very sorry they had to move, but there was no other choice. Alice Mae cried. She even threw a temper tantrum, although she had only had a tantrum once before and wasn't very good at it. Her parents looked at each other and went into the den to watch the news.

Alice Mae grew tired from kicking and screaming. She called her grandparents, who would do anything she wanted, but they said she would make friends at her new school and everything would be just fine.

Alice Mae's mother helped her pack up the things in her bedroom and told her what a nice bedroom she would have in the new house they had picked out.

Her father told her the house had a big backyard, and when summer came, he was going to build a playhouse for her and she could have her friends over. Alice Mae was happy about that and a little excited to see their new house, but she was still very sad when it was time to say goodbye to her teacher and friends.

She started at her new school in the second week of December. All the kids knew each other, and Alice Mae felt left out. The teacher told the kids to play with her at recess and play time. But all she could think about were her friends at her old school.

By the end of the week, two girls named Jodie and Jill, who were in her reading group, asked Alice Mae to sit with them at lunch and play with them at recess. The three girls quickly became best friends. Before she knew it, Alice Mae learned all the kids' names and decided she liked them all.

One afternoon, Jodie and Alice Mae were invited to Jill's house to play. Alice Mae's parents were happy that she had made friends quickly.

When Alice Mae came home, she told her parents about the decorations and the large tree at Jill's house. Jodie and Jill were talking about Christmas and how much fun it was and how the whole class would have a Christmas party.

Alice Mae didn't know much about Christmas, but she had an idea. She would have a Christmas party and invite her whole class!

She told her parents at breakfast that she wanted a Christmas party and to invite all her classmates. Her parents exchanged a furtive glance.

Her mother said, "Maybe it would be better to have a party in January. Perhaps there will be snow, and you could make snow angels and a snowman, and we'll have hot cocoa with marshmallows."

"No," Alice Mae insisted. "It has to be a Christmas party. Everyone is excited about Christmas. And we have to have a tree with decorations and lights and presents. Please, Mom. Pretty please. I'll be good, and I'll help."

Alice Mae's mom looked at Dad.

Dad said, "Well, Alice Mae. Christmas is a good time for people who celebrate Christmas. But, we don't. We're Jewish."

"What's Jewish?" asked Alice Mae.

Her parents each took a turn trying to explain what being Jewish meant. They used a lot of big words that Alice Mae had never heard and finally, they just said, "We'll think about it!"

To Alice Mae, whenever her parents said "We'll think about it," that meant they would probably do it. By the end of the school day, she had convinced herself that her parents were going to let her have a Christmas party. In fact, at the end of the day, when the teacher gave the final announcements, Alice Mae raised her hand and said, "I'm having a Christmas party at my new house, and everyone is invited!"

All the kids clapped, and Alice Mae was so pleased with herself.

"Wow!" said the teacher. "Are you sure everyone is invited? And when will it be?"

Alice Mae realized she didn't know the details, so she said, "My mother said you should call her!"

Alice Mae's mother was very surprised that evening when the teacher called and thanked her for hosting a Christmas party for the whole class. "It's such a kind thing for you to do. Just let me know the details, and I'll contact the other parents."

Alice Mae's mother and father talked in their bedroom for a long time. They had decided the night before that they would let her have a party, but wouldn't call it a Christmas party. When they told Alice Mae, she only heard that she could have it and, of course, she believed it would be a Christmas party.

Alice Mae was excited. She told her parents they needed a tree with decorations and presents because that's what Jodie and Jill had told her. When her parents said they didn't do Christmas trees and presents, Alice Mae pointed to all the neighbors' houses in their new neighborhood, which were decorated.

"Everyone does it," insisted Alice Mae. "This is what we do."

Dad brought home a tree and decorations, and Mom, who loved to shop anyway, really enjoyed buying a present for each child. The parents had contacted Alice Mae's mom and offered to bring snacks and Christmas cookies and told her about some games the children could play.

Two days before the party, Alice Mae rushed home with new information. They had to have a Santa Claus. It was too late to ask the real Santa Claus, but maybe Daddy could dress up like Santa and pretend to be him.

"Oh, no," Dad told his wife and daughter. "I will not be Santa Claus!" Then he saw the look on his wife's face. Every time he saw that look, he thought to himself, *I love you so much, I would get the moon for you!*

It was uncanny how his daughter had inherited that very same look. It filled him with so much love for his wife and daughter he could not deny them anything. He sighed. "All right," he groaned. "I'll be Santa."

His wife glowed and Alice Mae jumped up and down jubilantly.

The party was a grand triumph. The decorated house was welcoming. The children got along, and the mothers who were there had a good time too. Alice Mae's mom was pleased to meet the other mothers and make new friends. Santa Claus was a smashing success, and after delivering the presents in a pillowcase, the kids all asked him to tell them a story. He made up a funny tale, and they all pretended they didn't know he wasn't the real Santa!

At the end of the day, Alice Mae and her parents sat on the couch, hugging each other, reliving the joyful event, and deciding this new home would be just fine after all.

Alice Mae did learn about her Jewish heritage, and she always loved the stories of her faith, especially the Hanukkah stories. She grew up and devoted herself to Judaism for all her life.

Now, even though she is in her nineties and her parents have passed away, on the night of Christmas Eve, she raises a glass of wine and remembers all her friends at her one and only Christmas party.

Nor'easter Coming; Party Canceled

Rebecca Sue lived in a tiny town on the coast of Maine over seventy-five years ago. Her dad was a lobsterman. Her mother was the organist at the village church on Sunday and gave piano lessons during the week. They lived in a little gray house close to the shore where her father kept his lobster boat.

Rebecca Sue was in third grade at the village school. She loved school and Sunday school and the Girl Scouts, and she took piano lessons from her mother too. Rebecca Sue enjoyed the spring, when they planted the gardens and hiked through the forest to find lady slippers and dogtooth violets and searched relentlessly for jack-in-the-pulpits.

In the summer, Rebecca Sue ran barefoot and enjoyed beach-combing at the cove. As summer turned into fall, there was so much to do, with school starting again and the garden ready for harvesting. There were tomatoes to can and cucumbers to pickle. Dad always brought home a bushel or more of apples. Rebecca Sue and her mother made applesauce, and oh, how they enjoyed hot apple crisp, apple pandowdy and apple pie!

Their relatives came for a big Thanksgiving dinner, and after that, Rebecca Sue and everyone she knew looked forward to the activities of Christmas. Dad always took her along to find a tree in the forest, and her mother helped her string popcorn and cranberries and make paper and tinfoil decorations.

The church always had a children's Christmas pageant, and everyone memorized a piece of poetry or verse to share for the occasion. Most of the kids were in the children's choir too, and some even played instruments. Afterward, there was a party with a present for each child under the Christmas tree, and everyone took home a box filled with candies, a piece of homemade fudge, and a popcorn ball.

The Girl Scouts always went to the old timers' home to sing carols and distribute homemade Christmas cookies and cards they had decorated.

On the last day before the long Christmas break, every class in school held a party. The teacher had the kids exchange names beforehand and, on the day of the party, everyone put a wrapped gift under the tree that cost maybe fifty cents, but no more than seventy-five. And it could be a homemade gift too.

During the party, the teacher said they would exercise their brains by playing games. They would have a contest to see who could find the most words out of the word "Christmas," do holiday crossword puzzles, solve number problems, listen to carols, and create art projects. They would exchange gifts and were given cupcakes, cookies, popcorn, fudge and candy. They couldn't eat them all at once, though. Each child received a bag for carrying the treats home.

Rebecca Sue was beside herself with excitement. She could hardly wait! The night before, she had put the wrapped gift in her bag, along with a jar of pickles as a gift for her teacher.

When Rebecca Sue woke up on the day of the party, she saw that snow had covered everything and was still falling. She ran downstairs, where her mother was listening to their radio. The announcer named the towns where school was canceled for the day.

"School is canceled? Oh, no, the best day of the whole school year and it's canceled!" Rebecca Sue was so disappointed.

Mom said, "You always enjoy having a snow day. It's an unexpected treat."

"Yes, Mom, but not on the one day when we play games and have a party and exchange gifts!" wailed Rebecca Sue.

Just then, her father came in and said the weather outside was not fit for man nor beast! "It's going to snow all day and overnight, and the roads are pretty slick too. It's not safe to go anywhere."

Rebecca Sue groaned.

She and her mother spent the day doing Christmas baking. They put Christmas music on in the afternoon and started a jigsaw puzzle. In the evening, the neighbor came with a message because Rebecca Sue's family didn't have a telephone. The principal had called and said all school Christmas parties would be held on the first day back in January.

The gigantic blizzard left mountains of snow. Rebecca Sue and the other kids in the neighborhood loved to play on the snowbanks and slide down the sides.

Christmas came and went. Rebecca Sue's relatives visited after the holiday and everyone had fun. She received new skates for Christmas, so she was delighted when the weather turned cold and the town square was flooded and groomed for skating. The new year came, and school would begin the next day.

Rebecca Sue's mother reminded her to put the wrapped present and jar of pickles in her school bag. Rebecca Sue did, but it just didn't feel right to have a party. The Christmas magic was gone.

She got on the bus though and was happy to see everyone.

When they got to school and lined up to go inside, their teacher led them to the classroom door and stopped. She told them they must step into their time machines. She pretended to get into a time machine and told them to do the same thing. They looked at each other, grinned and played along. She said they were going back to last year—to December. It was the day of the Christmas party. She led them into the classroom...

It was magical. The shades were down, and the lighted Christmas tree stood in the middle of the room. It had all the decorations they had put on it before the big blizzard. The teacher told them to put their gifts under the tree, then she put a record on and they sang Christmas songs. All day long, they exercised their brains with all the games she had planned for the party. They exchanged gifts, and the teacher gave them treats she had made especially for them.

At the end of the day, with their treats and gifts in their school bags, she led them outside and had them step out of their time machines and welcome the new year. They got on the bus and talked all the way home about the best Christmas party ever.

Rebecca Sue grew up and moved away from that tiny town on the coast of Maine. But she always remembered the lesson she learned from the Christmas party in January. Holidays and celebrations are never about the date on a calendar, but always about the people you're with and the things you do.

Part 4: See the USA in a Roadtrek

The following stories are accounts of my experiences traveling around the country in my 1998 conversion van motor home called a "Roadtrek." I owned it for twenty-two years and appreciate all the happy memories of being a nomad. The stories remain.

Procuring a Roadtrek

The year was 1998. I had relocated halfway across the country from Concord, New Hampshire, to La Crosse, Wisconsin. My twenty-year marriage had dissolved, and I was on the cusp of a new life. I was pleased to have a teaching position at Viterbo University, but knew I would miss my family, who all lived in Maine.

As a seasoned camper, I was intrigued by the small, van-like motor homes I saw at area camping shows. I fell in love with the smallest made-for-one camper, the Roadtrek 170 Popular. Driving to Maine in a camper was the most cost-effective way to travel. I knew I would feel safe in a Roadtrek since it was self-contained. I could lock myself in and had my cell phone for communication. The fatherly salesperson at the camping show sealed the deal for me. He said he had a single daughter about my age, and he would be comfortable having her travel in this vehicle.

I found a dealership in St. Paul, Minnesota, and ordered my Roadtrek over the phone. The plan was that when it arrived, I would take the bus from La Crosse to St. Paul, where the dealership owner, George, would meet me and acquaint me with the Roadtrek. Then I would drive it back home.

The day came. It was the first week in June, and the Wisconsin weather was inviting campers to enjoy the outdoors. I took the afternoon bus to St. Paul and spent a few hours taking copious notes of everything George told me. When we finished, night had fallen, and it was time to drive the Roadtrek home.

George asked, "Have you ever driven a vehicle like this?"

"No," I admitted.

He looked worried. "Do you have any questions for me?"

"Yes," I said. "Could you please back it out of the garage for me?"

He smiled, jumped into the driver's seat, and backed it out. When I got behind the wheel, he asked, "Anything else?"

"Yes," I replied again. "Could you point me to the highway?" (I hadn't bothered to tell him I had no spatial intelligence whatsoever!)

He pointed. "Turn right, go a half mile, turn left onto the highway. You'll see the sign."

I thanked him. Then, after an awkward moment, he said, "Take your time. Get to know this van. It's a state-of-the-art machine and everything works. You'll get used to it."

I appreciated the advice, and I think it made him feel better too.

Turning right out of the parking lot, I had no trouble getting on the highway. I was careful and took my time. Traffic was not heavy. The Roadtrek was easy to drive, and I felt comfortable, so I increased my speed. About five minutes later, a car came up from behind and passed me. I noticed the driver was waving his arm at me, signaling me to pull over. Then I realized the driver was George. So I pulled over. When he came to my driver's window, I asked, "George, are you checking up on me?"

"Well, I was a little worried when you left. But I've been following you, and you seem to be doing fine. There's something else, though..." George hesitated.

"What?" I wondered aloud.

"Hmm... Well... hmm... You see... You forgot to pay me!"

"Oh! I'm sorry. You're right!" I reached for my purse and took out the bank check I had brought for him.

He looked relieved. We said our goodbyes, and I drove into what would become a twenty-two-year odyssey with my Roadtrek.

> Little Roadtrek, I love you.
> Little Roadtrek, indeed I do.
> In 1998, you were shiny and new.
> I only wanted to get away with you.
> You're just the right size, and with mindful thought,
> I laid down the cash and my Roadtrek I bought.

Single Female Traveling Alone

I got used to the Roadtrek quickly and took many adventures with it through my many years of ownership. For eleven years, I traveled from Wisconsin to Maine every summer to visit my family. I explored every possible east–west route, giving myself permission to get lost and not beat myself up about it.

Before I had a GPS, I pored over maps and planned my routes. However, as every road warrior knows, a construction project, a hidden sign, or heavy traffic can cause a wayward trek, sometimes for many miles.

I like to say that, because my spatial intelligence is limited, I have inadvertently seen much of this country. Fortunately, I have a robust curiosity, which offsets this limited spatial intelligence. I have found some of the most interesting places when traveling on the wrong road! I figure that every road goes somewhere, so I will end up somewhere, and that somewhere could be quite delightful.

A favorite activity of mine when entering a small town or city is to park the Roadtrek and walk from one end of the town to the other and back again. It's a healthy physical break from driving, and I've discovered lovely gardens, parks, libraries, bookstores, antique shops and coffee shops along my walking route. I've perused community bulletin boards and noticed what is important to a town. It's Americana at its best!

I'm always surprised when I am greeted by campground owners and fellow campers who express awe that I am traveling alone. People say things like, "You don't have a cat, dog or husband?" I quietly chuckle at the thought that a cat, dog and husband would be categorized together, probably as "pets."

I have been asked if I carry a gun or pepper spray, yet I have never felt the need to do so. Having been alone for a long time, I have learned to always know my surroundings, stay at family campgrounds rather than unsupervised Walmarts or out-of-the-way parking lots, be knowledgeable about the area, and keep my doors locked and my cell phone handy. I have not traveled this country in fear, although I am aware that I enjoy white privilege.

One year, I went to Iowa to visit the Amana Colonies for a few days and checked into the huge campground closest to the most populated colony. My campsite was sandwiched between two huge deluxe motor homes with slide-outs and patios. One was thirty-two feet, and the other had to be forty! My little seventeen-foot Roadtrek was minuscule between these two monsters.

As I was hooking up, I could hear some folks on the patio on the other side of one mega-palace discussing my tiny van. One said he would have to sleep in the fetal position. Another said it looked like a toy. Still another said one would have to stand in one place because there was no room to turn around.

I felt insulted and hurt. I think the Roadtrek felt insulted too. I quietly murmured, "Don't worry, Little Roadtrek. You look good!"

As the afternoon passed into the dinner hour, I fired up my two-burner gas stove. I sautéed garlic, onions and shrimp for scampi. I made rice pilaf, asparagus and a healthy salad. I put the tablecloth on the outside picnic table, brought out my CD player with classical music, poured wine into the wine glass, arranged my salad and dinner plate on the place mat, and, yes, lit a candle.

A few minutes later, I saw a couple of the earlier speakers casually walk by my campsite. Then I heard one say to another, "That's where that smell was coming from. God, it smells good. She's dining with music and candlelight and glass dishes!"

Another said, "We have a fancy schmancy kitchen with all the appliances, and my wife has never used it. We always eat out or get takeout!"

I gloated, enjoying every morsel of my meal. And I could tell my Roadtrek was happy too.

> Little Roadtrek, I love you.
> Little Roadtrek, indeed I do.
> Don't be afraid of those other big rigs,
> With thirty-foot bodies and luxury digs.
> They look big and fancy and always flashy,
> My little Roadtrek is tiny but classy.

Stormy Weather

The Roadtrek and I have traveled in all kinds of weather. Of course, I have never relished the thought of traveling in foul weather, and I've used common sense, but Mother Nature has a way of putting us amid storms and other inclement weather before we realize it.

One summer, I traveled from Wisconsin to South Dakota to visit the Black Hills National Park. Early in the trip, I was en route to Mitchell, South Dakota, where I had reservations at a campground and was looking forward to visiting the famed corn palace. The day was hot, with gray clouds and a warm, strong wind. It occurred to me that it seemed like tornado weather, but what did a native Mainer know about tornadoes?

I arrived at the campground late in the afternoon, and when I checked in, the attendant told me that tornado warnings had been issued for the area. She told me what county I was in, so I could follow the warnings on my radio. She said that if the sirens sounded, I should go to the cement block restrooms, which served as their tornado shelters.

I settled in, kept my radio on, and before retiring for the night, filled my backpack with my purse, my phone, my medications, a bottle of water, long-sleeved pants and shirt, and a hat. I figured that if I had to go to a shelter and a tornado took my Roadtrek into the sky, I wanted to be somewhat prepared.

I fell asleep in my clothes but was awakened suddenly by a pounding on the door. Sirens were screeching. The manager yelled, "Everyone, go to the restrooms!"

I jumped up, grabbed my sneakers and backpack, and joined the rest of the campers in the restrooms. I talked with a few people, most of whom who were from the Midwest. Parents carried sleepy children. Families huddled in small groups. I was clearly overdressed, most being in their hot summer sleepwear. Few had a backpack or bag with them. They assumed the sirens would stop, they would return to their campsites, and the danger would pass. One young mother told me the sirens went off a lot during the late summer—it was such a nuisance!

Hmm... I wondered, *I suppose folks would get used to the siren warnings and not take them seriously, but what about the one time it is serious and a tornado descends? Many wouldn't be ready.* It made sense that a Mainer, naïve about tornadoes, came to the shelter ready for mayhem and destruction. I wondered how these same folks would react to a nor'easter or blizzard.

On another occasion, in late September, I traveled to Iowa for a weekend of camping. The weather looked good for Friday and Sunday. Saturday's forecast was gray and rainy, but that was okay. I had a great mystery novel awaiting.

Saturday turned out rainier than expected, and I spent the day in the Roadtrek, reading and listening to shows on National Public Radio (NPR) and storytelling CDs. In fact, it was still raining when I went to bed.

At 4:00 a.m., I awoke to a pounding on the door. The manager yelled that the campground was being evacuated because the grounds were flooded. I jumped up, hurriedly dressed, secured everything, then hopped outside to disconnect the electricity and water, stowing the cords securely in their compartments.

At last, I jumped into the driver's seat, started the engine, turned on the lights, and saw a large puddle in front of me. *Oh, dear*, I thought. *This is serious.*

At the surrounding campsites, folks were dashing about, stowing the chairs and camp gear they had left out. I was grateful the Roadtrek was self-contained and easy to pack up!

I looked to the left and the right. There was no higher ground. The only way out was through the puddle. I drove forward carefully, praying it wouldn't be too deep. Once I started, I knew I needed to keep going lest I get stuck. That is a commonality between driving in snow and driving in deep water.

I kept moving ahead, slow and steady, and was relieved when the tires reached higher ground. I continued to the campground office.

Inside, other campers had gathered, and we were offered hot coffee. Some folks had radios, while others relayed information from phone conversations. A local convenience store brought in breakfast pizzas and doughnuts. Finally, a state policeman came in and reported on the road conditions throughout the area. He indicated that the major roads in the area were not passable.

After his announcements, I asked him about the route I had been planning to use to return to La Crosse, Wisconsin. He told me that the road had been washed out and was closed. The only available route, as far as he knew, was a long, circuitous one that would take me into Minnesota, where I would need to proceed north to Rochester and travel the highway east into western Wisconsin.

I decided to try it, knowing I might encounter roadblocks. If I had to wait for roads to reopen, I could always hunker down in my Roadtrek because I had battery backup.

As I followed the circuitous route, the rain stopped, and I saw numerous flooded yards and fields. It took a few hours, but I finally reached Minnesota, headed north, and arrived at the highway that went into Wisconsin. As I approached the highway, the area was familiar to me. I had been here before and knew exactly where I was.

I was relieved. The sun was out now. The early morning anxiety slid from my shoulders. Everything was all right. In fact... In fact, I remembered that just across the highway was the Rochester shopping mall.

Yes, shopping!

I went shopping and put the storm behind me.

> Little Roadtrek, I love you.
> Little Roadtrek, indeed I do.
> Through floods and tornadoes and dark stormy nights,
> We've always survived these terrible frights.

Finding Paul Newman

It was on a chilly but sunny day in January 2016 that I checked in at a campground for two nights in Los Cruces, New Mexico. I had never been to this area, so I was looking forward to a day of exploration.

The next morning, I filled up my fanny pack and my pockets with the essentials, like my phone, keys and money, and then set off to explore the city on foot. I enjoyed the entire day. It was cool, but the sun felt good, and I always appreciate the chance to walk after long driving days. I poked around in boutiques and antique shops, stopped at a local deli for lunch, and read all the historical markers along the way.

After spending much of the day walking, my feet were complaining, and I felt cold. Spying a Barnes & Noble bookstore, one of my favorite haunts, I went in to have a hot coffee, sit for a while, and warm up. I couldn't leave without browsing the aisles of bargain books.

As I was browsing, I noticed a teenage boy and girl in my peripheral vision giggling, teasing and engaging in typical teen boy-girl behavior. Evidently, the girl had an item that the boy kept trying to get away from her. They engaged in this hide-and-seek chase throughout the aisles, with much giggling and teenage glee.

I ignored them and continued my quest for the bargain of the century when I turned the corner at the same time that the boy took the corner at high speed, with the girl in close pursuit.

The collision was inevitable. We smashed into each other, and because he had the greater speed, he pushed me into a bookshelf behind me. I felt a pain in my derrière and realized I had been knocked into the sharp corner of the bookshelf. I lost my balance and sank to the floor. I know I didn't hit my head or pass out, but I must have closed my eyes.

When I opened them, I was looking into the most beautiful blue eyes of the most handsome Adonis I had ever seen. *It must be Paul Newman*, I thought. *It must be. And we're together. Forever. Just the way it was always meant to be!*

Of course, it wasn't Paul Newman, but a nice guy with blue eyes who saw me get knocked over, knelt beside me, and kept patting my arm, saying, "Don't move. Stay still. Don't move."

Okay, I thought, as I looked up at him adoringly.

I heard a voice on my other side. Turning my head, I saw a young woman with a concerned look—and when I saw her name tag with "Manager" on it, I knew why she was concerned. This could be a lawsuit waiting to happen! She knew she had to document everything and get it right for her incident report.

She asked me what happened. I told her I bumped into a young man—I looked around and saw the two teens looking at me nervously. The boy looked scared, and the girl was biting her nails. I pointed to him and told the manager we had collided.

The boy's expression seemed to say, "Oh, no! I knocked down an old lady! I'm so grounded! My life is over. I will never be able to pursue my dreams!"

I knew this was just an accident. The manager didn't have to worry. I wouldn't press charges. But, of course, she didn't know that and continued to console me, get me water, and monitor my physical status.

In those few minutes, though, I must confess that I enjoyed delivering a multi-minute stare at the teen, glaring at him for his childish play. Somehow, in those few moments, all the rage I ever felt toward the behavior of the teenage boys in my teaching career came forth in that glare!

Of course, it was the only punishment I would exert. After all, he was in a bookstore, and as a professor of education who specialized in literacy, that was a redeeming feature.

Then I turned again, gazing up at Mr. Adonis with the beautiful, blue eyes. He was still patting my arm. I said I thought I could stand, and I'll always remember how lovingly he held onto me and helped me up. The manager gave me a glass of water and placed a chair next to me.

There was an awkward moment as we all were caught in a tableau. The teens fidgeted nervously as I flung one more glare toward them. Adonis continued to look concerned, and I smiled at him. The manager took charge, taking everyone's names, and then they left.

I looked longingly after Adonis, but he walked out of the store and out of my life. I assured the manager I was fine, although I could feel the pain in my rear and knew I would be sore for the next few days. She wanted to call somebody, and to avoid alarming her by telling her I was traveling alone, I said I wasn't far from where I would be spending the night.

I got up to leave, and—*ouch!*—I instantly realized this was going to be uncomfortable! I returned to the campground and gathered plenty of ice for my bottom. The next morning, I broke camp, got into the driver's seat, sitting on a mound of ice, and left Los Cruces and Adonis behind.

Little Roadtrek, I love you.
Little Roadtrek, indeed I do.
Then, on one winter day in the great southwest,
Wham, bam, alakazam!
My aching body came to you for rest.

A Birthday Celebration

On my birthday, in January 2016, I was traveling toward Amarillo, Texas. I checked into a KOA campground late in the afternoon. The attendant asked me if I needed information about the area or restaurants.

I told her, "It's my birthday, and I thought I might take myself out to eat tonight if there's a nice place nearby."

"Oh, your birthday!" she gushed. "You have to go to the steak house. They have good food and music, and if it's your birthday, you get a free meal." She seemed very enthused about it.

"How far away is it?" I asked.

"Just a mile down the road. They even have a chauffeur service and will come to pick you up. I'll call them." She picked up the phone, asked me if 5:30 was okay, and spoke into the receiver. "This is KOA. Ms. Blackstone would like to be picked up for dinner tonight at 5:30 at site D-24. It is her birthday." She put the phone down and declared, "It's all set!"

"Well, I guess I'm going to dinner at a steak house tonight," I said to myself.

I settled into the campsite, and as the pick-up time approached, I freshened up and changed my clothes. Exactly at 5:30, I noticed a sleek black limo enter the campground, complete with a huge pair of steer antlers attached to the front. "This should be interesting," I thought.

The limo lumbered up the road and stopped at my campsite. I stepped out of the Roadtrek and was greeted by the driver, who looked for all the world like Hoss—you know, Hoss from the TV show *Bonanza*!

Hoss, I thought. *It's Hoss. I love Hoss. This will be all right.*

He helped me into the back seat, and we made small talk as he drove to the restaurant. He dropped me off at the front door and said he would be waiting for me when I was ready to return.

I looked around. The restaurant was more than a restaurant. There was a collection of buildings connected to the huge establishment. The various shops housed a casino, riding apparel, ice cream, candy, hot sauce, old time photos, western jewelry and souvenirs.

I was escorted to my table in the large, relatively empty dining room. But it was early and a weeknight. I could imagine how lively the place would be on a weekend or later at night.

The waiter wore the traditional cowboy outfit, complete with cowboy boots, a Stetson and lots of fringe. The clothes hung from his tall, lanky, young body, but he attempted to play the role of a friendly cowboy.

He showed me the birthday menu. I ordered, then enjoyed looking at all the cowboy artifacts on the wall.

A young woman with the title of "Manager" on her name tag, but not dressed in cowgirl apparel, chatted with me and discreetly asked to see my license. She checked my birth date to assure herself I was a legitimate beneficiary of their kindness.

I savored the meal, accompanied by my favorite wine, and for dessert, ordered the hot fudge sundae. As I was wondering if anyone would notice if I licked the ice cream dish, a roaming cowboy band came in and proceeded directly to my table. They serenaded me with cowboy tunes and sang "Happy Birthday." When they were done, they went on their way, and I chuckled to myself about the whole experience while finishing my freshly brewed coffee.

Completely satisfied, I thanked my server, browsed in the other shops for a bit, then headed to the front entrance. There was Hoss in the limo with the steer antlers on the front, watching for me. He helped me into the car, and we chatted on the return trip. He left me at the door of my Roadtrek and wished me well.

I stood in the center of the Roadtrek for a few moments recounting the experience, then chuckled to myself and said, "Yee-haw! Happy birthday to me!"

Little Roadtrek, I love you.
Little Roadtrek, indeed I do.
You've carried me, my stories, books and bike,
Toted all my possessions to wherever I like.
While finding my bliss with each day's ride,
We've traveled this country, far and wide.

Part 5: Teaching Stories

I was privileged to serve as an educator for forty-three years.

For all of those years, I found that storytelling was my preferred teaching tool, probably because the human brain is wired for narratives. The stories here came mostly from classroom experiences that improved my teaching and became insightful for the teachers I trained. A few others grew out of experiences at conferences and other professional settings and emphasized the importance of reading and comprehension.

The Interview

Note: This fictionalized story of an interview for one's first teaching position is a useful discussion starter when helping novice teachers prepare for the challenge.

I am so nervous. I have been nervous every moment of every day since the superintendent's office called five days ago to schedule this interview. Now that I am here, in my car, in the parking lot, I think I might be sick. No, no, no. I won't be sick. I will get out of this car now, go into the building, and ace this interview.

Well, maybe I won't ace it. Maybe I'll just survive it. If I do survive it, I will apply for a permanent position at Wendy's. A career at Wendy's might be nice. Not!

I get out of the car, smooth my skirt and my hair, and go into the building. The large black letters on the door say, SUPERINTENDENT'S OFFICE. I push open the door. My eyes go to the counter. No one is there. Oh, no. What do I do now? I stand, glued to the floor. A matronly woman appears from the backroom and says, pleasantly, "Hello. How can I help you?"

I squeak out my name. She smiles and nods. "Have a seat," she says. "Dr. Witzel is on the phone right now, but he knows you are coming and will be with you shortly."

I sit in one of the four aqua-colored office chairs. I look around and see a rack with educational flyers and brochures. On the coffee table, I notice last month's edition of *Educational Leadership*, a copy of *Parents Magazine*, and today's newspaper.

I wipe my sweaty palms on my skirt in anticipation of having to shake hands with Dr. Witzel. I wonder what his first name is. Oh, I think I have to pee. No, I don't have to pee. I peed a half hour ago. Oh, no. Maybe I do. Something is wrong with me. I think I might throw up. Where would I throw up? I spot a plant in the corner. Yup, if I feel like throwing up, I should throw up in the plant's pot. I move two chairs closer to it.

"Settle down," I say to myself. "Think of something else." I try to remember the questions I should ask. Let's see. Do we get Martin Luther King Day off? My boyfriend wants to know if the health plan will cover birth control pills.

I reach up to adjust my glasses and touch my chin. Oh, no. It's a zit. It's a super big one. It's growing. It's probably all red too.

I hear the door open and footsteps. "Hello, Ms. Blackstone." Dr. Witzel sticks out his hand, and fortunately, I remember to shake it. "I'm glad to meet you. Follow me." We go into his office and he motions me to a chair in front of the desk while he takes his place behind it.

He smiles at me. "I know you've been interviewed by the principal and some of the teachers. They speak highly of you. I have a few questions for you too."

They spoke highly of me. Yahoo!

He continues, "Our school district believes in the constructivist theory of teaching and learning. Briefly, what is your understanding of the constructivist theory and how would you implement it in the classroom?"

I take a breath. "You're on!" I say to myself. "Stand and deliver."

"I have studied different theories of learning and teaching, and I too believe that the constructivist theory is valuable when teaching students in the twenty-first century. The constructivist theory claims that learners construct their own knowledge; that is why the teacher must not just stand and deliver the knowledge. The teacher gives the information, then provides time in which students can use the information, mold it to related information already in the brain, and construct new knowledge for themselves.

"In the classroom, I must engage students in active, not passive, strategies, by which they take information, work with it, fine-tune it, and relate it to knowledge that already exists for them. I will do this by having students secure information for themselves after I give them a framework. I will have them work collaboratively with their classmates to create knowledge, because we know that learning is a socially mediated activity."

He is smiling and nodding affirmatively. I think he's impressed. I nailed it! I hope...

"Thank you. It seems that you have a good understanding of constructivist theory," he says. "Now, I know the principal and teachers asked you about your strengths. I'm wondering about your weaknesses. What would you consider to be your greatest weakness?"

I'm on a roll now. I can't fail. I had not anticipated this question, so I blurt out my response. "That's easy. My biggest weakness is pepperoni, mushroom and extra cheese pizza! Another weakness is Uncle Richard's chocolate nut cookies. They are to die for!"

His eyes grow big, and he smiles. "That's interesting. I meant, what would be a weakness related to teaching?"

Oh, no! What a doofus! I can't believe I said that. I am so embarrassed! No time for embarrassment. Now is the time. I have to answer. He's looking at me. Answer the question.

"One weakness, of course, is that as a new teacher, I know I don't know everything and I need to keep learning. I'm also nervous about behavior management, and I told the teachers in the interview that I would appreciate any help they could give me. I also know that I am not an early morning person and being at school by 7:30 every morning will be a habit I will have to develop. But, I have had several 8:00 classes, and in my student teaching experience, I had to be at school by 7:15, and I developed a way to do that. I got into the habit of having my teaching bag and lunch, even my clothes, ready the night before. For a while, I set two alarm clocks and put one across the room. These things worked for me, and I intend to keep on doing them."

He is smiling. "It's good when teachers know themselves well," he says. "Do you have any questions for me?"

I continue. "I have learned how important it is to work with parents and the community agencies, especially when a child might be having a problem. What are the opportunities and programs you have for parent and community involvement?"

"That's a good question."

He likes my question!

"We have several programs, and you'll find them all in this handbook." He passes a thick document to me, entitled *Policies and Programs*.

He stands, and I take this as a signal that the interview is over. "Based upon your credentials and the recommendations of the principal and teachers, I am pleased to offer you this position. My secretary will make sure you receive all the forms and information you need. Congratulations. Welcome aboard!"

My heart throbs. I got the job! Wahoo! I've got a job! Wow. I leave his office. The secretary hands me a manila envelope. It's labeled "New Teacher's Welcome Packet." She tells me it contains all the information I need and instructions on completing the forms. I am to call her if I have any questions. She smiles and congratulates me.

I leave and head to my car. I feel like doing a dance. I think I'll treat myself to a hot fudge sundae. But first, I have to pee!

I Have to Talk to Them?

My first teaching position was at the old Nash School in Augusta, Maine. It was a small neighborhood school right behind the state office building. There were four classrooms ranging from kindergarten through third grade, four classroom teachers, and a teacher's aide. One teacher was also the principal.

I taught first grade and loved my new profession and all the activities it entailed. I loved planning lessons and putting up bulletin boards. I loved the children. It never occurred to me they all looked like me and most likely engaged in similar cultural customs to those I knew from my family and childhood. I had a lot to learn about cultural diversity in the forty years ahead of me!

During that first fall in 1970, I was pleased with myself. Then, in late October, the principal announced that parent-teacher conferences would be held in early November on a half-day, and we should strive to meet with every single parent. I froze! Parents? I had to meet with the parents?

Somehow, the whole concept of parent-teacher conferences escaped me during my teacher preparation days. I probably heard it mentioned but didn't think about it, preferring to think of lesson plans and how to teach elementary topics like reading and math.

My college program did not offer a course on how to work with parents or the community. Later, in my master's program, I developed a passion for the topic and eventually wrote a dissertation on it.

But in 1970, I was scared. Why? I was in my early twenties. I assumed most of my students' parents were older and more mature and had more experience. Who was I to talk to them about the education of first graders? Plus, I wasn't married and didn't have children. Heck, I didn't even have a boyfriend!

Fortunately, a more experienced teacher showed me how to organize information and conduct a conference. I was skilled at organizing. That was no problem. I had a folder for each child that contained samples of their work and notes on what I wanted to tell the parents about their child. The notes were invaluable in keeping my thoughts organized.

I was so nervous about conducting my first conference, and I must say that, even though I got used to it, I never became completely comfortable conducting parent-teacher conferences, especially when I had to relay information parents didn't want to hear. Thank goodness I didn't have to face culturally diverse parents during those first years. All that experience and knowledge would come later.

Since that first year, I have learned that most parents are just as nervous about meeting teachers at a conference, especially new parents with young children. I have been grateful for opportunities to study the dynamics of parent-teacher conferences. The insights from these studies have allowed me to develop programs to help teachers overcome the anxiety of meeting with parents.

The core insight I learned and freely share with others is this: Every child is a representative of a family. To receive a child is to receive their family.

The Phonics Game

I learned to read because of two natural abilities. First, I was a "goody two shoes" who always paid attention and did whatever the teacher said, and second, I had an excellent visual memory.

In first grade, I remember the small reading group, the tall teacher, and a large flip chart featuring Dick, Jane and Sally. (This was the 1950s. Dick, Jane and Sally were the characters in a popular instructional reading program.) The teacher pointed at individual words in the sentences and said them, after which the students repeated them. Then, the teacher would repeat the process, showing individual words in isolation, and students repeated them to ensure that they could identify the individual words. Having a superior visual memory and an ample speaking vocabulary, I quickly acquired a large sight vocabulary.

In second grade, I encountered a teacher who used another strategy to teach reading. This was phonics, a term I learned as an adult in a teacher preparation course. She was keen on phonics, or sounding out words. She put us into small groups, showed us letters and groups of letters, told us the sounds they made and had us repeat the sounds after her.

In my eight-year-old mind, I saw this as a game; one I did not particularly enjoy. But I loved this teacher, and if this was the game she wanted to play, I would participate.

When it was my turn to look at a word and repeat the sounds, the teacher gave me several opportunities to say them, again and again. Of course, I was oblivious to the fact that she asked me to repeat because I wasn't getting it. I concluded that she gave me many turns because I was her favorite student! In fact, I announced to my mother that I was my teacher's favorite, and when she asked why I thought that, I gave as proof that the teacher gave me more turns than anyone else!

During my teacher preparation program, I learned all about phonics and sounding out words. It is a useful technique for teaching children to decode words. But it didn't work for me, and it hasn't worked for thousands.

Teachers must have many strategies at their command to meet diverse learner needs. This anecdote also shows how children often interpret actions in the classroom through an emotional lens.

Three Nice Ladies

Becoming literate requires much time and instruction. Consider how long it takes for an average child to learn to read and write. They start in kindergarten, most coming to that first year of organized school with some basics, like knowing their name, some letters, some words and some book-handling knowledge. Usually, by fourth or fifth grade, most children have mastered the basics of reading and can read independently. For the rest of their school years, they will use reading to enjoy literature and acquire knowledge.

Many times, this normal, upward trajectory can be disrupted by problems in the family, sickness, emotional stress, instruction that does not match the child's learning style, or a combination of these factors. A child can lag bchind and will need help to catch up with the class. Schools have many programs to help children catch up, but a child's progress will be impeded if these programs are not consistently used.

Jason was in third grade, and he was already behind in his reading. His parents requested extra help. In addition to his regular classroom instruction, he would receive support from a Title 1 teacher and a conscientious parent volunteer. ("Title 1" refers to federal funds given to schools to help low-income school systems meet the educational needs of their students.) Jason even had some one-on-one time with a high schooler who came weekly to listen to him read. Everyone hoped that with this extra help, Jason's reading would improve, and he would soon catch up to the rest of the class.

But after three months, Jason's reading performance wasn't improving. The teacher referred him for a comprehensive reading assessment by the research lab at the state university. The assessment center was directed by Dr. Erickson, a professor of education with expertise in diagnosing literacy problems.

Early in the assessment, Dr. Erickson interviewed Jason to learn how he viewed his reading problems. She asked, "What do you do if you come to a word you don't know?"

Jason had an immediate reply. He answered, "I do what the nice ladies tell me to do."

This was an unusual response, and Dr. Erickson discussed it with Jason's teacher. She learned Jason had at least three, and sometimes four, nice ladies who helped him with his reading. When he came to a word he didn't know, his teacher asked him to think about a word that made sense with the rest of the ones he'd read. His Title 1 teacher asked him to break the word apart. His volunteer tutor asked him to sound out the word. The high schooler gave him the word.

Dr. Erickson concluded Jason was confused by these different strategies and was not creating an independent strategy for figuring out words. His reading instruction was not congruent. Jason needed to have consistency in his instruction and to develop independence.

Over some weeks, Dr. Erickson met with the school personnel and Jason's parents, who all helped him with his reading. They learned Jason could not improve if his instruction was disjointed. They worked together to create consistency in their instructional approach.

It took some time, but Jason's reading did improve, and today, he is a voracious, independent reader.

Julius Caesar

I was a victim of a very poor teaching practice in my high school freshman English class. Of course, I did not know it was a poor teaching practice until many years later, but I offer the story to inform teachers everywhere.

My English teacher distributed William Shakespeare's play *Julius Caesar* to our class in September, announcing this was the first book we would read that year. He prided himself on his strict curriculum policies and grading practices. He announced that, at each class meeting, a two-question quiz would be given about the homework reading. I didn't have to be good at math to calculate that a two-question quiz could only yield three grades: 100 percent, 50 percent or 0 percent.

I was always conscientious about homework. But as I settled in to read the daily readings, I was confused. I had read many books, but this one differed from any I had read before. The language was weird! I couldn't figure out the plot. I could barely keep track of the characters. I reread it several times but couldn't understand this mysterious work.

Of course, I failed the two-question quizzes with either 50 percent or 0 percent for some consecutive days. After each quiz, the teacher discussed the homework reading, and by concentrating on the classroom instruction, I began to get a glimpse of what this book was all about.

Near the end of the book, I understood more and even aced a few quizzes. I was so glad when it was finished and the class moved on to other readings and to topics more familiar to me.

So, being an adept reader, why couldn't I comprehend this text? I lacked the background knowledge that could assist me in comprehending it or for understanding Shakespearean literature. I had never encountered the language used by Shakespeare. I didn't have any knowledge of the culture or context of the period.

There was nothing wrong with me. But there was something wrong with my teacher's strategy. He disregarded his students' need to have background knowledge to bring to a reading situation. He didn't know the ABCs of background knowledge: Access background knowledge; Build knowledge that is lacking; Correct misleading or incorrect knowledge.

Shame on the teacher if he knew this concept but didn't put it into practice.

Gertie Mae Johnson

On May 3, 2002, Gertie Mae Johnson almost lost her job. It was not the first time she had lost a job. She'd had several jobs in her thirty-two years. She didn't almost lose it because she was incompetent, lazy, using drugs or untrustworthy. She almost lost her job because of her limited literacy skills.

Gertie Mae was born into a pretty average, middle-class family. Sure, there were problems in her family, but what family doesn't have problems? Her dad was in the Navy, and their family moved from base to base until Gertie was a young teen. After getting out of the Navy, her father relocated them to a small town in central Ohio, where he got a job in an auto repair shop and her mother got a job as a cook in the local school district.

Gertie was the second of four children. She always did okay in school. She never failed any of her classes, but her grades were never stellar. Reading was hard for her. She fell behind somewhere in the primary grades and never quite caught up. Maybe it was because she changed schools a lot and never had a consistent reading and writing curriculum. Maybe it was because her older sister brought home the high grades and, more than once,

Gertie Mae heard her parents and teachers say, "Why can't you be more like your sister?" Maybe it was because nothing she read really appealed to her.

Other problems began during middle school. Gertie Mae became pals with classmates who were like her. That is, she related to the kids who didn't do well with reading assignments. They understood her and praised her for things she could do well, like run track, do gymnastics, and play softball. She spent almost all of her time with her "tribe," as she called them.

Gertie Mae loved being with her tribe all through high school. After all of those years of moving so often and having to make new friends at every new school, Gertie loved having a consistent group of friends. They endured the long days of classroom instruction, proceeding from one boring subject to the other, never really understanding the concepts presented. They lived for after-school activities and spent evenings at each other's houses, doing a bit of homework and a lot of goofing around! Gertie graduated, barely, and got a job doing assembly work at a paper mill.

It was at the paper mill that Gertie met Ernie, her future husband. He had just finished his tour of duty in the Navy and said he was ready to settle down. They had two children in the first three years of marriage. Things were hard financially. Gertie didn't know babies could be so expensive!

She tried to keep her job at the mill, but childcare took the major chunk of her paycheck. She and Ernie began to argue a lot, both about the kids and doing work around the apartment. He had an affair with an office worker at the mill, and a few months later, left Gertie for good. He was always late with child support payments, and on a few occasions, she had to contact the courts to get the payments.

Gertie tried to do the best she could. It was a relief when her younger sister suggested that Gertie and the kids move closer so the family could help care for her children. What a relief! Gertie found a job working for a company that cleaned offices in the evenings. And her sister took care of the kids while she worked.

Gertie's job at the cleaning company was going well. She liked her coworkers. She did a good job, and her supervisor often complimented her for being a hard worker. So Gertie was surprised when her supervisor asked her to come into the office for a meeting.

The owner of the company and Gertie's supervisor were waiting for her at the meeting. The owner was very direct. He said that while he appreciated her hard work, he was close to having to let her go.

Gertie couldn't believe it. Did she hear right? She was stunned. "Why?" she asked. "What did I do wrong?"

The supervisor said her job was in jeopardy because of her poor job performance.

"Poor job performance! How can you say that? You've told me I've done a good job!" Gertie couldn't believe it. What was wrong here?

The supervisor continued, "Yes, Gertie, you do a good job at cleaning, and I have complimented you on that. But we have had complaints that you haven't followed instructions from some of our clients, and they have asked us not to send you to their offices anymore. I have talked to you about those complaints before and this just can't continue."

Gertie remembered. There were things about her using the wrong furniture polish, not setting up a conference room the right way, and not moving anything off a table, but those were just petty complaints made by rich professionals who complained about everything.

The supervisor continued. "Mr. Richards left a note asking you to set up a conference room for eight people with flip charts and marker boards, and you ignored it. You didn't do it. Mr. Dudley left a note asking you to not touch anything on his desk because he was working on a big project with an approaching deadline. You straightened the desk anyway, and he was livid when he had to reorganize all of it. And he missed the deadline! And Dr. Thomas said he left you a note not to use regular furniture polish on his new and expensive imported coffee table. You ignored that note too—you used the regular polish, and now he has unsightly stains all over the table. Do you see what we mean by poor job performance, Gertie? You can't just ignore what our clients ask of us!"

Gertie remembered. She had seen written notes, but she never paid attention to them. And even if she had seen them, she probably wouldn't have been able to read everything on them. She began to cry. She understood now.

It doesn't matter if you're a good person or even a diligent employee. You have to be literate to hold down a job. In fact, you need to be literate to do so many things. She remembered all the times she had to rely on others for information. Perhaps it was time to reconsider going to the tutoring center to get help with her reading.

Teaching Alex

I was still a novice teacher when I accepted an invitation to tutor a student in an adult literacy program. Alex came to my home every Monday evening for our lessons. He was in his thirties, had a full-time job with a masonry company, a lovely wife, and two young children. He initially sought tutoring because his children wanted him to read to them, a request that tugs at every parent's heart.

At our first session, Alex told me about falling behind in reading in elementary school; during middle school and high school, he never really caught up. He did get some extra help, but it wasn't enough, and he graduated from high school with rudimentary reading skills.

He got a good job as a manual laborer that required only minimal reading skills, and he was a hard worker. But when his young preschool children brought library books to him to read, he could read some of the words, but not all. And he knew that the children, as they got older, would bring more advanced books that would be too hard for him to read.

Alex did have some reading skills. He had a basic sight word vocabulary and a great deal of comprehension. Because Alex came to every Monday session with stories of what he and the family did over the weekend, I used the time-honored strategy of the Language Experience Activity with him. Alex dictated his family's experiences, and I wrote them down. That dictated text then became the teaching tool. Because this was his own experience and these were his chosen words, he could read it more easily.

I pulled individual words and phrases from the text to examine them for phonics and word-building skills. The best part was that Alex took it home and read it to his family. This created a habit.

Every Tuesday morning, his children looked for Dad's story on the breakfast table. They especially enjoyed finding their names in the adventures they had together.

In May, on the Monday after Mother's Day, Alex excitedly told me about finding a Mother's Day card for his wife. He recounted that when he took the children to pick out cards, he noticed one that said, "To my wife..." He had never known there were Mother's Day cards for wives. He found one he could read and was pleased to present it to his wife.

Alex taught me a critical lesson about teaching an adult learner: use printed materials from real life. The learning materials for adult learners include greeting cards, menus, shopping ads, workplace literature, newspapers, magazines, hobby manuals, flyers, leaflets and religious materials, as well as, in the 21st century, the specialized offerings of the internet.

Buddy, the First Grader

Note: This story is a recollection from a retired gentleman who reminisced about a traumatic experience in first grade. I have told it from the child's point of view to emphasize how he felt. Teachers and parents must consider how personal relationships can play out negatively in the classroom.

Buddy sat up straight and tall and looked around. His sister Lizzie had said that first grade was important, and he had to work hard to please his teacher. He was ready. He saw his cousin Rita a few rows away. He knew some of the other kids and hoped they would play with him at recess. But right now, the teacher, Mrs. Langley, was talking.

She said she would give each of them a paper, and they should write their letters neatly and perfectly. He could do that! Easy peasy! He knew all about letters. His mother had taught them to him, and he had practiced them with Lizzie and Rita.

When he got his paper, he chose his best new pencil and started right away, working slowly and carefully to form each letter. He was so engrossed he didn't even notice when Mrs. Langley stopped by his desk and inspected his work. Buddy looked up, smiling and expecting Mrs. Langley to be pleased.

But, no. Mrs. Langley was frowning. She looked mad. She grabbed his paper, ripped it up and said, "Start over. And this time, do it the way I said to do it!" She gave him a new piece of paper.

Buddy was stunned. *I was doing what she said*, he thought. *Why is she mad?* He looked around to see what others were doing and saw that they were making the letters like he had. He started again, working slowly and carefully. He was halfway done when Mrs. Langley asked a student to collect the papers, and they were all dismissed for recess.

A few days later, Buddy was working on his numbers paper. He loved the numbers paper. He knew about adding too, and Lizzie was showing him how to do take-aways.

Buddy was afraid of Mrs. Langley, but his mother said he had to do what the teacher said and work hard. On this particular day, Buddy felt a growing need to go to the bathroom. He tried to ignore it. He didn't want to ask Mrs. Langley for permission to go to the bathroom. But after some time, he couldn't wait any longer and raised his hand. He saw Mrs. Langley look right at him, but she didn't call on him. He kept his hand in the air and waved it around. But she never called on him.

The rule was that if you needed something, you raised your hand. You didn't get out of your seat or call out in class. Buddy didn't want to break the rules. That would make Mrs. Langley really mad!

Buddy's need to go was getting urgent. He stood and shifted from foot to foot. He wiggled. He squirmed. But the teacher didn't notice. Then it was too late. He could feel warm liquid flowing down his legs and into his socks. Looking down, he saw a wet stain on the front of his pants. He watched a stream of liquid form a puddle under the chair.

Buddy was so embarrassed. He didn't dare look around to see if anyone noticed. His eyes filled with tears. He didn't want to cry, but he couldn't help it. He sat in his seat, put his head down on his desk, and cried softly into his arms.

Later, he heard Mrs. Langley say it was time to go home. She handed out papers, and when she got to his row, she saw the puddle. "Buddy, what happened?" she asked in a loud and accusatory tone, which made all the others look. "Why didn't you tell me you needed to go to the bathroom?"

Buddy said, "I raised my hand. I even stood and waved it. You never saw me." But Mrs. Langley had already moved down the row.

October came and everyone was excited about Halloween. Buddy and his sister could hardly wait. They each had new masks and costumes. Their father took them to the usual places to trick or treat—the homes of their grandparents, their aunts and uncles, and neighbors.

When they got to a house, their dad stepped behind a tree and the kids took turns ringing the doorbells. They would say "Trick or treat" and oh, they were collecting lots of candy in their pillowcases!

The last house they went to was a big, humongous building. Buddy had never been there before. He ran up the walk and rang the doorbell. The door opened, and Buddy's eyes got big. It was Mrs. Langley. This was his teacher's house! He had never even thought about Mrs. Langley living in a real house. Did his father know this was her house?

He then noticed his father was right behind him, not behind a tree. His father was looking right at Mrs. Langley and smiling. His father said to her, "These are my kids! I bet you're surprised."

Buddy was shocked. He didn't know his father knew Mrs. Langley. But Mrs. Langley looked mad—just like she did in school sometimes. She put something in each of their bags, then shut the door!

He looked back at his father. Now his father looked mad and said, "Let's go!" They got into the pickup truck and traveled the back roads to their home. They were silent all the way home.

Buddy was a young adult when he inadvertently learned that, years earlier, his father and his teacher had had a romantic relationship that resulted in bitterness and strife. He never knew all the details, but he did learn the universal truth of this teaching story: Teachers, don't seek revenge on a student's parent, lest you scar that child for life!

Hypertension

Jim and Arlene Hutchins had been married for forty-nine years. Next year, they were going to have a big family gathering to celebrate their golden anniversary. The years had been good to them. They had three attentive children and seven beautiful grandchildren. They had worked hard, he as a carpenter and she as a hairdresser. They were enjoying their retirement—gardening more, volunteering at the food bank, and attending their grandkids' school activities.

They were fortunate to have pretty good health, except for the usual consequences of aging. Arlene had arthritis in her knees, while Jim had high blood pressure. He also had cataracts that interfered with his driving, but he was scheduled to have them removed in two months. They were both being treated for high cholesterol.

On Tuesday, Arlene drove Jim to the walk-in clinic to test his blood pressure and update his medication. When he checked in, the nurse took him into an examination room and took his blood pressure. She said the doctor would be in shortly.

The doctor came in, reviewed his chart, and said, "Yes, your hypertension is an issue. I will give you a prescription." They stopped at the pharmacy on the way home and filled the prescription.

At home, Jim set the new bottle next to his other medications on the kitchen shelf. Each morning, he took a pill from each bottle.

A couple of weeks later, Arlene was up early and noticed Jim take a pill from each bottle. "What are you doing?"

Jim looked at her in amazement. "I'm taking my pills. One for my blood pressure, and the other for my hypertension."

"No, Jim." She took the bottle away from him. "Hypertension and blood pressure are the same thing. You need only one pill a day."

He looked surprised. "They're the same thing? Why didn't anyone tell me?"

Arlene panicked as she realized Jim had been overdosing on the medication. She called the clinic to tell them—and to remind them that medical terms can be confusing.

Take on an Empty Stomach

Shasita sat at the kitchen table in her small apartment in New York City. She was so tired. It was all she could do to make breakfast for her two girls and get them off to school. Her husband left early for his trucking job. Her stomach pains were coming back again. She should have gathered up the dirty laundry and walked down to the laundromat at the corner, but she was just too tired. All she wanted to do was go back to bed. The laundry and dirty dishes would just have to wait.

She woke with a headache around two o'clock. Her stomach pain was not as bad. She got up, opened a can of soup, put it in the microwave, and sat at the table. Maybe if she had something to eat, she could get some chores done before the girls got back. She put some rice and chicken in the Crock-Pot for dinner.

By the time the girls got home, Shasita felt better. She had dressed and washed the dishes. The girls always were excited after school. They loved their new school in America, and their English was getting better every day.

Shasita reminded herself to call the English as a Second Language (ESL) office at the school and sign up for English classes too. But she wanted to wait until she felt better.

After supper, her stomach pains returned, and she laid on the couch while the girls did their homework. She heard her husband come in from work and got up to heat his dinner. As she took it from the refrigerator, she felt dizzy. She held on to the counter. Pain went through her stomach and she doubled over, which was how her husband found her.

"Shasita, what's wrong?" He collected her in his arms and guided her to the couch. She recounted her day. He said she had to go to the walk-in clinic tomorrow. She reminded him they didn't have this card—this medical insurance card. It was too expensive to see a doctor. He said he didn't care. He could work overtime to get extra money. He insisted she promise to go the next morning.

Shasita was able to walk to the clinic the next morning. She couldn't understand what they said, for they all spoke English. But she showed them where the pain was in her stomach. The doctor gave her a paper for medicine and a card with a date and time for her next appointment. The nurse walked her to a place with medicines, where a man took the paper, then gave her a bottle with some pills. She returned home.

She looked at the bottle but couldn't read the words. She would wait until her daughters got home. Her older one was in fourth grade and could read almost anything. As soon as they got home, her daughter read the words slowly. "Take one tablet in morning on an empty stomach."

On an empty stomach? What did that mean? She asked her daughter. "What does 'on an empty stomach' mean?"

"I don't know, Mama. I've never heard that before."

Shasita wondered all day what the instructions meant. Did it mean she should lie down and put the tablet on her stomach?

Was that how it would help the pain? That seemed like a strange thing to do. She had taken medicine in her country before but never heard about taking it on an empty stomach.

Her husband looked at the medicine bottle when he got home. His daughter helped him read it, and he had never heard this phrase before either. He took the bottle downstairs to the landlady. She was American. She read the bottle and explained what taking a pill on an empty stomach meant.

He understood now and smiled, thanking her many times. Returning to Shasita, he explained it meant to take the pill before she ate breakfast.

Many months later, Shasita was in her ESL class. The teacher said they would study idioms. Shasita had never heard of idioms before. She listened carefully as the teacher explained and gave several examples. Other students offered examples too.

Shasita raised her hand. "I think I have one. Take on an empty stomach. Is that one?"

"Yes," said the teacher. "That's a good example of an idiom."

Shasita told them in faltering English about the medicine bottle and thinking she should lie down and put a pill on her stomach for her pain. They all laughed.

She would have to tell this story to that nice doctor and nurse someday.

Dear Imperfect Florence Nightingale

Living with loved ones through declining health and negotiating the labyrinth of nursing home procedures is difficult for any family. While my family was fortunate to have healthcare providers who cooperated with us in every way, the path was bumpy. My oldest sister led our family through our parents' nursing home experience. She modeled the procedure, so when I had to negotiate the nursing home path for her several years later, I knew what to do.

During a period of frustration, I expressed my aggravation to my dear friend and storyteller/poet comrade, Dr. Michael Seliger of Orangeburg, New York. He took my spoken frustrations and wove them into a beautiful poem. We offer the poem to others who may need to remind novice healthcare providers gently that each elderly patient was once an active, vibrant person.

Dear Imperfect Florence Nightingale...
Thank you for all that you do.
Each touch, each turn, each moment
Of bringing sunshine to my eyes,
Food to my lips, cream to my skin.
You are the vital link
That carries me forward
In this world, before I leave
To take my turn in the Next.
Your skilled hands perform tasks,
And you know you've done them well,
Professionally,
And I know that too,
And I am grateful to you.
It is not in your job description,
But I do wish you could do a little more...
Sing to me, tell me a story,
Pour out a small part of who you are
That might remind me of who I used to be.
Look into my eyes and smile
As you turn my weakened body
From side to side...
You may never quite see it,
But when I see you finding joy
In any little thing,
Or putting extra love into your touch,
It truly makes my heart sing,
And brings my past and future
Closer to these moments
We know as The Fleeting Present...
Fondly,
Your Patient

Part 6: Pandemic Ponderings (2020–21)

In March 2020, upon the arrival of COVID-19 in Maine and by order of the Governor, I began my shelter-in-place odyssey. During the following months, I adapted to my new way of life, like other humans on the planet. Whenever I ventured out to buy groceries, go to the post office, and run other essential errands, I wore a mask, practiced social distancing, and pretty much kept to myself. I found my communities from church, storytelling and writing on Zoom. As the weather improved and limited gatherings were sanctioned, I met one or two friends at a time in the park for picnics. As fall and winter weather descended, I surrendered my desire to travel to warmer climes, hunkered down, and was grateful for my Zooming opportunities. The following stories were born of my sheltering experiences while observing the pandemic and the political chaos of that year.

Quarantined

In mid-March 2020, I was sitting in my apartment. Due to the COVID-19 pandemic, residents were being asked to quarantine themselves. Quarantine... Shelter-in-place... Self-isolate...

Hmm, I thought to myself, *I am seventy-one years old, and I have never been quarantined. This is a new experience for me. I wonder what this adventure will be like!*

I reviewed my life and that of my family, beginning in early 1940s. My sister Ruth and I were not even born yet. My parents had five children at the time, ages three to ten, and were busy caring for an active family and earning their livelihood on their potato farm. But one day, life brought a new challenge.

Their second child, Barbara, who was then eight years old, contracted scarlet fever, a highly contagious and dangerous disease. The county health commissioner declared that the family should be quarantined and posted an official quarantine order on the farmhouse door. My mother had to keep Barbara apart from the other four children and make sure contagions did not get passed to the healthy children.

My father stayed at his parents' home. Perhaps this was fortunate, because being on the outside, he could deliver groceries and necessities to the family.

I wonder what it was like for my thirty-something mother to juggle the tasks of caring for a sick child and tending to four healthy children, while not having the support and help of her husband and fearing the disease would spread if she was not diligent.

This quarantine occurred at a time without television, video games or internet. She coped with laundry using a wringer washing machine and clothesline, and managed the household without a dishwasher, microwave or prepared meals.

In this 2020 quarantine, I found myself raising a toast to my mother, who lived through a time of quarantine that must have challenged her mothering skills and brought fear to her mother's heart.

By the early 1950s, I had been born and was already five years old. I loved to go to Sunday school, where I sat, arms entwined with my friend Patti each week, while listening to our teacher, Miss Lucy, tell a story from the Bible. Afterward, Miss Lucy distributed the Sunday school paper, which had the story in print for someone to read to us during the week and a picture to color.

Miss Lucy would put a box of nearly new Crayola crayons on the table. I called them the Sunday school crayons because they were like new, with pointy ends and paper still intact, unlike my own crayons at home, which were broken and tattered. Patti and I colored, trying to stay within the lines and completely enthralled with the moment.

One Sunday, Patti wasn't at Sunday school, and she wasn't there the next week either. When I asked my mother if I could go to Patti's house, she explained that Patti was very sick and wouldn't be coming to Sunday school for a while. I wasn't allowed to visit her because I might catch her illness. She said Patti had polio, and when I asked what polio was, she explained it as best she could. I was sad, but I noticed something else too. I sensed that my mother was very scared that I or my siblings would get polio like Patti.

Next came the early 1960s. Ruth and I were in middle school. One day, my mother happily told us we would go that evening to the church basement to get the polio vaccine. When we arrived, a uniformed nurse took our names, ages and address, and we were welcomed into the assembly hall. We saw long tables set up with white paper coverings. Trays and trays of sugar cubes covered the tables.

The polio medicine was contained within the sugar cubes. We joined a line, and when it was our turn, we each took a cube. My sister put her cube in her mouth right away. I looked at my cube, searching for the medicine. The center of the cube was a reddish, orangey, yellowish color. *That must be the medicine!* I thought. I popped it into my mouth, then wondered all the way home if I would feel anything, like a side effect.

Wouldn't it be great if the COVID-19 vaccine came to us encased in a gummy bear or a chocolate treat?

The pandemic of 2020 inserted itself squarely in the midst of Eastertide, Passover and Ramadan. A commonality of these religious observations is the invitation to the faithful to come apart—to come away from the busyness of life, to remember the stories of the faith.

During this pandemic, my heart reached out to those for whom life had been thrust into chaos, fear, daily battles and sleepless nights. I knew the new narrative of their lives was disturbing and might continue to disturb them for a long time to come, even after the virus was no longer contaminating our bodies.

It was almost with a sense of guilt that I recognized that for many of us, the pandemic was our opportunity to come apart, to practice solitude, to reflect and to restore. It seemed like a shame to re-emerge from the pandemic and not have grown mentally, emotionally and spiritually.

I resolved to live in the moment during the pandemic and gather all the good I could from it. I hope the same was true for you.

And when we gather again, face-to-face, we will say, "I survived. Let me share what I learned."

The Game of Life

Do you remember the board game called Life? It was a fun pastime that turned life into a game. You spun the wheel and moved your car along the track of life, paying bills and growing your family along the way.

I've been musing about how the COVID-19 pandemic was like other games and activities we enjoy.

The pandemic was like playing dodgeball. We were all afraid of that huge, moon-like orb with prickly sticklers that we saw on the television screen. We frantically kept our distance, moving this way and that, never getting into another's way, and constantly keeping our eye on that unpredictable, insidious ball.

At times, the pandemic was like rowing a boat. We felt safe inside the boat even though the murky virus swirled around us. But we rowed, both oars in the water, maintaining balance as we moved toward safer ground. Sometimes the virus seemed peaceful, and we took a much-needed pause from the hard work of rowing. We looked around, enjoyed the beauty of the landscape, and nodded encouragingly to those in other rowboats. Then the virus ocean became angry and seemed intent on upending us, and we hunkered down, rowing furiously and deliberately. Our arms—and our bodies—tired of rowing. But we continued, knowing that it would build strong muscles for whatever lay ahead.

Then there were other times, when the pandemic reminded me of playing freeze tag, where someone is chosen as "It," and if you are tagged by It, you must freeze. In one version of the game, if you are frozen by It, another player with unfreezing powers can unfreeze you, and you may continue to play the game. In the spring of 2020, the Great Gamer of the Universe shouted, *Freeze*! And all the nations of the world froze.

What did they do in their frozen states, collectively and individually? They looked around for those who could free them. They used their voices, gestures and advanced technological inventions to seek help. A harmful virus swirled around them, but they continued, reaching out in all directions.

Then, an interesting thing happened. While in their stuck-in-place frozen vigil, they noticed, beyond the swirling virus, other swirling viruses of racism, injustice and violence. Repulsed, they fought from their frozen states. Whenever the universe was going to return to its pre-game status, they wanted to play in a world that accepted and respected all peoples.

But wait! Isn't there supposed to be a coach? Where's the coach? Isn't there supposed to be a referee? Aren't we supposed to be abiding by the rules and playing the game with determination?

For me, the spirit of God is the coach and referee. For you, it may be something else. But in the end, we're all doing the best we can to stay in the game.

Jigsaw Puzzles

I love jigsaw puzzles. During my childhood, my whole family did them together. In my adulthood, I was reminded of my love for puzzles by my sister Barbara. When I visited her, we worked on one together, sometimes engaging in idle chatter, and other times, in companionable silence. My best memories are those times we engaged in deep, intimate conversations that bonded us together in sisterhood as we worked, piece by piece, to create a beautiful whole.

Now that I am alone, I work on jigsaw puzzles sometimes to keep my hands busy while listening to a movie, music or stories. Many times, I've worked in silence, mentally sorting through a problem and seeking a solution.

I wonder why I am so enamored with jigsaw puzzles. Perhaps I see them as problems to be solved, knowing the solutions are in my hands if I am patient and thoughtful and work piece by piece.

During the pandemic, I shopped online for puzzles and found they were scarce. The sale of puzzles and other toys increased significantly, and I was met by the words "Sold Out," "Back-ordered," "Unavailable" everywhere I looked. Who would have thought that jigsaw puzzles and toilet paper were the most sought after commodities of modern times!

I love to start a new puzzle. When I open the box, I see all the pieces that will eventually become the interesting picture on the cover. I know there are just enough pieces to make the picture. There are no leftovers to be discarded or that aren't needed. Every piece is important to the final product. No single piece is more important than another.

I look at the individual pieces, many of which are not that pretty. A piece may have multiple colors that don't blend well together or it may be all one color and give no hint how it is connected to others. Some are brightly colored and invite the puzzler to pick them up. They may start with those pieces but are eventually forced to deal with all the ones that are not so pretty or easy to place.

I like to start by finding all the edge pieces to build the framework. Then I know the boundaries and have a sense of the locations of different parts of the puzzle. Knowing boundaries is a good thing. Stretching boundaries can be a good thing too if one is being creative. But completing a puzzle is more of a visual discrimination task than a creative exercise.

Once I start the inside part of the puzzle, I realize one important principle. Each piece is connected to other pieces. And those pieces are connected to more until the picture is complete. The puzzler's task is to make connections, one piece at a time.

Another principle is that some pieces will not fit until others are put in place. These pieces must be set aside until their connections are made clear. There is a right time and place for each piece to fit into the whole.

Puzzles can come alive with surprises. One can stare at an ordinary piece many times, be baffled about its placement, maybe even think it belongs in some other puzzle, and when it is finally put into place, the puzzler exclaims with delight at discovering its unique position in the picture.

Could it be that jigsaw puzzles are a metaphor for life? Our lives are made up of individual pieces representing people, places and experiences. Some are aglow with color and others are dull and drab. But all the pieces are connected. Parts of the puzzle may be more difficult to build than others, and some must be set aside to be dealt with later. Yet all people, places and experiences are included. There are no wasted parts. At the end of life, the completed puzzle speaks to a life lived.

Consider the personal life puzzle each of us is constructing. All the pieces will fit together, even though they often seem random and unrelated, and constructing the puzzle seems so difficult. May you and I, the puzzlers, practice patience, endure the difficulties, seek solutions, find connections, and realize contentment as we assemble the picture that portrays our uniquely beautiful lives.

Weatherizing

The pandemic of 2020 dictated that I refrain from traveling to warmer climes during the winter of 2021, so I prepared to settle into my little Maine apartment for the winter. I assessed what I needed to do to make life more comfortable during the months ahead. One project I knew would be helpful was to place plastic over the four large windows of my apartment to keep the rooms warmer and save on fuel.

I watched multiple online videos about how to complete this project. After seeing several well-dressed, white-haired ladies with manicured nails winterize their windows, I was convinced I could do it too. I visited my local hardware store to examine the supplies and found a kit that included enough plastic and two-sided tape for four windows. *Just right!* I thought. *Easy peasy! What could go wrong?*

On the appointed day, I gathered the materials: plastic, two-sided tape, scissors, measuring tape, a hair dryer and a large glass of wine. I measured and cut the plastic to fit the first window, and unrolled enough tape for the top of the window frame. This is when the project became troublesome.

I quickly discovered that sticky, two-sided tape takes on a life of its own when unleashed from the roll. A small piece stuck to my sweatpants and, in trying to get it off, I inadvertently unrolled another yard or two. Somehow, the tape circulated around my body, and I was trapped in the clutches of sticky tape! As I fingered the tape, it twisted, morphing into long strings that took flight every which way!

I swallowed a gulp of wine and proceeded, valiantly placing the plastic and securing it with tape. When I was done, the window was covered, but it sure didn't look pretty! Over half the tape was lying in strings on the floor, and the wine glass was half empty!

The second window wasn't any easier. I assumed the two windows were the same size and didn't realize they were different until I had wrestled with the sticky tape and secured the plastic. I had to discard the plastic, along with more tape, and start again. By the time the second window was done, it didn't look much better than the first, and the wine glass was empty.

I realized I needed to make another visit to the hardware store. This meant tackling the other two windows when I had built up a reserve of courage. When I purchased the second set of supplies, the same do-it-yourselfer handyman cashier who had sold me the first window kit said, "You needed more supplies?"

He knows! I thought. *He knows I really suck at this project and am so inept I need to start over again!* But what came out of my mouth was, "I've done all the downstairs windows. I think I'll do the upstairs and maybe even the attic." I picked up my items and confidently exited the store.

On another day, I gathered the essential materials and a large glass of wine and tackled the remaining two windows. They did get covered with plastic that day, but not without some wrestling of the tape, cursing and frequent sips of wine.

All in all, I completed the project. The windows didn't look that good, so I did what any homemaker would do. I bought new curtains to hide my mistakes.

My God!

I believe in God.
I pray to God.
My prayers are sincere.
I have faith that God cares about me
and receives my prayers with love.
I watched several videos of the insurrection at the United States Capitol in early January 2021.
I was appalled.
I was angry.
One video stopped me cold.
The rioters were inside the Senate chamber.
They sat in the seats of senators.
They verbally mocked these servants.
They rifled through desks.
They took photos of papers.
They overturned furniture.
Then, one rioter hollered, "Let's pray!"

Others agreed and formed a circle.
I inwardly chuckled as one removed his cap,
holding it to his chest in reverence.
All rioters bowed their heads as the leader prayed.
I did not hear what was said in the prayer.
I watched.
I was silent.
I was aghast!
Then, I reacted!
Wait a minute!
Hold your horses!
Stop the presses!
This is *my God!*
They were praying to *my* God!
"What does God think about this?" I wondered.
Surely God must be angry...
But if my God receives my prayers with love,
surely God must show them the same favor.
God is not a magician, but created unique individuals
with all that is needed to make decisions and choices.
What is God thinking in this moment of my angst?
Perhaps God is thinking, "Boys, boys, boys...
You're headed down a dangerous path.
There will be consequences to suffer."
When I pray, I wonder if God thinks,
"My daughter, you should think this through.
There will be consequences to your choices."
I think of the senators,
cowering under tables in a nearby room.
I imagine some of them were praying too.

Praying to the same God who was being invoked in the Senate chamber.

Praying to *my* God!

Praying to the God of the rioters!

What does God think of all this?

Part 7: Hope

The following stories pay homage to hope as the attribute that lies dormant deep in our souls until we need to access it and put it to work.

Whispering Hope

When I was in fifth grade at Harpswell Elementary School, my sister Ruth was in the eighth grade. It was spring, and while I was excited for school to end, Ruth was looking forward to her eighth-grade graduation.

One evening at the supper table, Ruth announced she would be singing a duet with another girl at the ceremony. This was no surprise since Ruth was very musical. She said she would be singing the alto part of a song entitled "Whispering Hope."

Graduation came and went, and the duet was absolutely beautiful, as were the music and words of the song.

> Soft as the voice of an angel,
> Breathing a lesson unheard,
> Hope with a gentle persuasion
> Whispers her comforting word.
>
> Wait till the darkness is over,
> Wait till the tempest is done.
> Hope for the sunshine tomorrow,
> After the shower is gone.

Whispering hope,
O, how welcome thy voice,
Making my heart, in its sorrow, rejoice.

The song was written by Septimus Winner, using the pseudonym Alice Hawthorne. Septimus, born in 1827 in Philadelphia, Pennsylvania, became a self-taught musician who could play a variety of instruments. As an adult, he formed a music business with his brother and other partners. He wrote two hundred volumes of music for more than twenty instruments. Some of his tunes are still known today, like "Listen to the Mockingbird" and "Oh Where, Oh Where, Has My Little Dog Gone?"

In 1868, Septimus published "Whispering Hope," and he was surprised that it became so popular.

The most famous story of hope goes back to the Greek myth of Pandora's Box. Pandora was a beautiful human woman. Upon her marriage, she was given a special jar by the gods and was told never to open it. But she grew curious and opened the jar. Out of it flew all the illnesses that would plague the world forever, like hatred, envy, greed, disease, poverty, pain, death and war. Pandora quickly put the lid on the jar, realizing what she had done.

When all was silent and still, she heard a tiny, tiny voice. Pandora didn't dare open the jar again, but the tiny voice was persistent.

"Let me out. Let me out! Please, let me out."

Finally, Pandora couldn't stand hearing that voice any longer and opened the jar. This time, a spirit called Hope flew out—a spirit that spread itself over all the world and has forevermore burrowed itself into the deepest part of the human soul.

Hope dwells within each of us. Hope inspires many of us to plant tiny seeds in the soil each spring. Hope is why storytellers keep searching for stories and for listeners to hear them.

Yes, *hope* is alive and well, way down inside the human soul. When pressure assails you, remember the words of hope.

> Whispering hope,
> O, how welcome thy voice,
> Making my heart, in its sorrow, rejoice.

Multiple Forms of Hope

The Middle School Language Arts Curriculum is very explicit about the structural analysis of words. It says, "The student will be able to identify, define and use root words (also known as base words), prefixes, suffixes, singular and plural noun forms, and past, present and future tenses of verb forms."

On day twenty-four of the school year, during the fifth class session on the structural analysis of words, the competent, conscientious Language Arts teacher wrote one word on the whiteboard: HOPE.

"Hope," she said. "What do you know about this word?"

"It's a noun," said one student.

"It can be a verb," said another.

"It can be an adjective if you add an ending like -ful to make 'hopeful,'" offered a third.

"Good start!" replied the teacher. "Given all you have learned about how words are structured, make a list of words using 'hope' as the root word."

Twenty minutes later, each student submitted a form of the word "hope" in turn.

Hopes: present tense of the verb or plural form of the noun.
Hoping: being in the process of the act of hope.
Hoped: the process of hoping is now done.
Hopeful: a descriptive word, being full of hope.
Hopeless: complete lack of hope.
Non-hope: same as hopeless.
Re-hope: to abandon hope, then regain it.
Dis-hope: to give up hope; also known as de-hope.
Mis-hope: to hope mistakenly.
Semi-hope: to hope partially.
Anti-hope: to be against hope. (Who would dare?)
Pro-hope: to be for hope.
Trans-hope: to spread hope across miles or populations.
Tele-hope: to spread hope through telephones or televisions.
Techno-hope: to spread hope through electronic technology.
Intra-hope: hope that resides within a person or community.
Inter-hope: hope that spreads between people and communities.
Hopia: the condition of living in perpetual hope.

"Fine," said the teacher. "Good work today. I am giving you three words for tomorrow. Think about them and prepare to tell us what they mean to you. 'Hope springs eternal.'"

Hello, My Name Is...

Note: I attribute this story idea to my sister Barbara, who was a dear and generous person. You have heard of people who tithe, that is, who give a percentage of their income to their church? Barbara tithed her vegetables. In the summer, when produce was abundant and friends gave her ample portions, she always set aside some to give to others. For Barbara, true giving was meant to be a chain reaction. Many times, when I visited and she offered the remaining cookies for me to take, I would say, "Oh, no. I can't eat anymore cookies!" Then she'd gently suggest, "Not for you. Give them to someone else." I couldn't help imagining a story about giving, where that simple act creates a chain reaction.

Hello, My Name Is... Phyllis

I think I did something important today. It was really just a little thing, but it seemed to help. I smiled at Sue—or at least that was what was printed on her name tag at Walmart.

She was the cashier in the checkout lane I chose. I had to wait quite a long time, even though I was second in line. The lady ahead of me gave Sue a really hard time. She was buying a tablecloth, and it turned out to be $15 more than she thought. She had Sue check it two more times.

When Sue kept giving her the same price, the customer insisted she found it in the clearance bin for $9.99. Sue said the item should not have been in the bin and maybe it was placed there by mistake. The customer thought she should receive the discounted price because the item was in the bin. When Sue refused, the customer asked to speak to a manager.

The manager arrived, heard the story from both Sue and the customer, checked the register, and announced that she was sorry for the confusion, but the item was the regular price. When the customer argued, the manager firmly restated the price. She groaned but handed over her credit card to pay for the item.

During this extended interaction, Sue nervously looked toward me and the few others behind me, and I could tell she was worried those of us in line would be exasperated. Once, I made eye contact with her and smiled reassuringly. She gave me a half-smile that seemed to say, "Please don't be mad at me for making you wait."

When the customer had paid, she grabbed the bag and huffed her way out.

When it was my turn, Sue said, "I'm sorry for the wait."

I smiled back. "No problem. You did the best you could."

"Thank you."

I assured her, "The rest of the day will be better."

Hello, My Name Is... Sue

A lady named Phyllis smiled at me today I only know her name because she wore a shirt that said, "I'm Phyllis!" Who does that? She told me the shirt was a present from her friends when she moved away. They all wore shirts that said, "Goodbye, Phyllis!"

I wouldn't have blamed Phyllis if she was mad and grumpy. The customer ahead of her was really difficult, and I had to call the manager. It was awful. When Phyllis stepped up and smiled at me, I felt so much better.

Late in the afternoon, I had an elderly customer named Eve. I know her name because her hands were gnarled, and when she tried to get her credit card, all the cards spilled from her wallet. I gathered them up for her and saw her name on one of the cards.

She kept apologizing for being so slow, but I told her it was okay. I could tell the customers in line behind her were getting aggravated by the old woman's slowness. I could hear their loud sighs. But, you know what? My job right at that moment was helping Eve.

I ignored the others. I helped her with her purse, made sure the bag was securely on her arm, and wished her a good day. I did the right thing.

Hello, My Name Is... Eve

A really nice girl named Sue helped me at Walmart today. I'm always so slow these days. My hands are crippled and ache most of the time. I hate being in a line because people behind me are so impatient. I had trouble taking my credit card out, then I got nervous and dropped all my cards.

Sue helped me find the right card, then collected the others and returned them to my purse. It didn't seem to bother her that people behind me were growing impatient. She focused her attention on me, and I'm so grateful.

When I got to my car, the sky was dark, and it started to rain—first a sprinkle, then a downpour. A lady and her two little girls were at the car next to me, and I could hear her on the phone. She had locked the keys in the car and was calling for help. When it started to pour, I asked if they would like to sit in my car until help came.

The girls got in the back, and the mom got in the front. The girls were talking about going to McDonald's for lunch. I asked the mom if they could have a cheese stick. My grandchildren love cheese sticks. When she agreed, I directed the girls to find them in my grocery bag and to each have one.

The mom was saying, "I should have known not to try to get so many things done in one morning. I always get harried and end up doing something stupid!"

The girls started telling me about themselves. One of them asked, "How *old* are you anyway?"

Her mother gasped.

I said, "I'm eighty-two!"

Their eyes widened, and the other one said, "I've never known anyone that old before!"

Within a half hour, the locksmith came, and they were on their way again. I'm glad I could help.

Hello, My Name Is... Frazzled Mother!

I should know better. Never try to do everything in one morning, especially when I have the girls with me. This morning, I was proud that things were going well, and I promised the girls lunch at McDonald's. Then, I locked my keys in the car! How stupid! And it was raining really hard.

A nice lady in the car next to mine asked if we wanted to wait in her car. It was a godsend. She invited the girls to each have a cheese stick and asked them about themselves.

I thought I would die when Alyssa asked, "How old are you anyway?" Thankfully, she didn't seem offended and said she was eighty-two.

Eventually, the locksmith came, and we were on our way to McDonald's.

The girls found us a table, and I went to the counter to order two Happy Meals. A girl named Kim took my order. She was young, about sixteen or seventeen. She looked awful. Her face was red and tear-streaked, and her eyes were puffy. She was obviously upset.

I'm in my thirties now, but I remember being that age. Some problems seemed like the end of the world. I reached out, touched her arm, smiled at her, and said, "Whatever is upsetting you, it will be okay." I usually don't do that kind of thing, but I just felt like it was the right thing to do.

Fresh tears formed in her eyes, but she looked right at me and said, "Thank you."

Hello, My Name Is... Kim

Something good happened today. Three days ago, I found out I was pregnant. And when I told my boyfriend, he dumped me. He said it was my responsibility to make sure this didn't happen and that he couldn't help me. He wanted to go to college and couldn't have a kid. I told my parents, and they were mad and upset and yelled at me. I've been crying for three days straight. I've been a mess at school and here at work, but I knew I had to keep going.

Today, this mother came in with two little girls. I had just finished a crying jag and must have looked a wreck. I could tell she noticed. After she placed her order, she gazed into my eyes, placed her hand on my arm, and said, "Whatever is upsetting you, it will be okay." Isn't that nice? I was so grateful.

And, later, my mother called and said she and Dad had talked about it. We would go out for a nice dinner tonight and find a way to get through this together.

Late in the afternoon, a lady came to the counter. She was wearing a shirt that said, "I'm Phyllis!" I suppose that was her real name. I noticed her sad appearance, which was like my own for the past three days. She had been weeping and looked so depressed. I could relate! So, I smiled and said, "Hello. How can I help you today?"

She looked so relieved and grateful.

Hello, My Name Is... Phyllis

Just when I think I'm getting over this heart-wrenching, broken heart thing, some little occurrence triggers it all over again. That happened today. It was the end of the day, and it had been a challenging day at work. It's exhausting to keep on working and holding my emotions in check all the time.

Anyway, I decided to stop at McDonald's for coffee. I always say, "The answer to life's problems is freshly brewed coffee!" When I stepped up to the counter, this young girl named Kim looked right into my teary eyes, gave me a big smile, and said, "Hello. How can I help you today?"

I sat down with my coffee and kept thinking about that sweet girl who had brightened my day. Then it came to me. Three gifts that are always appreciated and are easily given again are welcoming eyes, a friendly smile, and thoughtful words. I should write a story about that!

Bundles of Hope

On the day before Christmas, Edward Emmanuel McAlister Jr. parked his truck in the driveway, lifted a large box from the back, and carried it up the back stairway to the master bedroom. He was returning from Waterville, where he had picked up the box of children's gifts from the Maine Children's Home.

This was a hard year for his family. Ed's lumber company had laid him off without health insurance, and there was no extra money for Christmas this year. His wife had noticed the ad in the paper about eligible families signing up for Christmas boxes. At first, Ed resisted, saying he didn't want to take charity. But his wife convinced him they had supported the Maine Children's Home in many ways in the past, and now they could use the help. He wanted his kids to have a nice Christmas and hated not having any money this year.

Ed peeked into the box. There was clothing for each of his three kids, an age-appropriate toy for each one, a board game for the whole family, books and some small items. There was wrapping paper and bows too. His wife would love that. She loved wrapping Christmas gifts.

Stashing the box in the closet away from prying eyes, he went downstairs to the kitchen, inhaling the smell of popcorn and sweet syrup. His wife and kids, including his son, Eddie (formally, Edward Emmanuel McAlister III), age twelve; and daughter, Emily, age ten; were scooping up handfuls of glistening popcorn and packing them into balls. But it was his youngest daughter, Melinda, age five, who had clearly taken charge of the operation.

Yes, she was a surprise, but they couldn't imagine life without her. He called her "Magpie" because she was always talking and directing the household.

"Hi, Daddy. We're making popcorn balls. You want to help? You have to wash your hands and be careful, the popcorn is hot with syrup on it. Doesn't it smell de–li–cious? I can hardly wait to eat one. But be careful! You could break a tooth. You know what, Daddy? Eddie, Emily and me made a play for tonight to show you and Mommy. It is hi–lar–i–ous. You will laugh!"

Ed exchanged a look of amusement with Karen, his wife. Magpie sure brought a lot of fun into their lives. And her older siblings were her willing minions and doted on her constantly.

Later, as he and Karen were looking through the Christmas box together, Ed said, "I wish I could give the kids a real Christmas."

"Ed, this is a real Christmas. These gifts are just right. The kids will love them. And we have the gifts my parents sent. Our kids have never had a super big Christmas. They have always loved what they received. And they always love the things we do as a family. Everything will be all right, I promise."

She was right, of course, but his heart was still heavy. Christmas was taken care of, and he was grateful for that. But there was the day after Christmas, the day after that, the rest of the winter and the entire year... He couldn't see the end of their financial troubles, and he didn't even want to think about other things that could go wrong.

He went to the woodshop and started a fire in the woodstove. His father had helped him build the shop before he passed, and now Ed had all of his father's tools. As a master carpenter, Ed's father had taught him some woodworking skills. Ed wished he had paid more attention.

He was trying to make a gift for everyone: a towel holder for Karen, a keepsake box for Emily, a trophy shelf for Eddie, and a doll bed for Magpie. His work was okay, but the gifts would've been so much better if his father had made them.

Sitting in the rocking chair next to the woodstove, Ed thought about his parents. After a while, he leaned back, pulled his cap down over his eyes, and slept.

Ed dreamed he was walking in a cave and there were thousands of bundles of all shapes and sizes around him. He met a woman in a long, flowing white dress and asked where he was.

"This is the Cave of the Bundles of Troubles, and I am the Keeper of the Cave."

"Bundles of troubles?" questioned Ed.

"Yes, every human carries a bundle of troubles on their left shoulder."

Ed looked at his left shoulder. She was right. There it was. He realized how heavy it was. How long had he been lugging it around?

"You can go into the cave and trade it for a different bundle, if you would like," the woman offered.

"Really?" Ed brightened. The idea appealed to him. So, he wandered through the cave, picking up some bundles and looking into others. Some bundles contained only one trouble, but a challenging one like homelessness, mental illness, or constant physical pain. Other bundles had several serious troubles, and Ed wondered how anyone could carry them. He finally returned to his own bundle. *I may as well keep this one*, he thought. *At least I know what it contains.*

As he left the cave, the Keeper of the Cave said, "Did you ever peek into the bundle over your right shoulder?"

Ed looked. He was surprised to find there was indeed a bundle on his right shoulder.

"That is your bundle of hope," the Keeper said. "Everything in that bundle can help you with your troubles."

He looked inside and saw his skills, his strengths, his experiences, his talents, his attitudes, his dreams, his opportunities, his ideas.

Ed woke from the dream. It had been so real to him. He thought about it throughout the rest of the day.

. . • . .

Christmas Eve was fun. Their home was alive with music, good food, a play that was hilarious, and a long list of holiday knock-knock jokes! Eventually, the house was quiet, the kids were in bed, and the presents were wrapped. After checking the doors, an exhausted Ed went to bed.

Again, Ed dreamed. It wasn't the Cave of Troubles and the Keeper of the Cave this time. Instead, it was a large grizzly bear chasing him. Ed ran, but the bear was upon him. His heart pounded. He could feel the bear's breath at his neck. Then, a bump—and *thud*! He opened his eyes.

Magpie had flung herself on top of him. "Daddy, Daddy! It's Christmas. Mom said you have to get up. She's making your coffee. We had hot cocoa. She said if you don't get up, she'll take a bite out of your cinnamon bun. Daddy, there are gifts under the tree. There's a doll bed for my doll. I put Dolly to bed in it. Be quiet, Daddy, so you don't wake her up. Daddy, do you know what's delicious? A candy cane in hot cocoa. Eddie put one in mine. I didn't think I'd like it, but it's delicious. Get up now, Daddy. I'm putting a candy cane in your coffee."

She bounded off the bed and out the door. Ed glanced at the clock—5:16 a.m.! He had better get up, rescue his wife... his cinnamon bun... and his coffee!

. . • . .

The entire day was nice. The kids were happy with their gifts, and everyone got along. Now, it was late afternoon. The older kids were busy in their rooms. His wife had convinced Magpie to take a nap with her. Ed stretched out on the sofa in front of the fire. It was so warm and comfy here. He closed his eyes.

Soon he was back in that horrible dream. The bear was sitting on top of him, and he could hardly breathe. He wondered how he could get rid of this load. He was so afraid. Then, in an instant, the bear was gone and instead his mother was there, comforting him in her arms.

He cried, "I'm scared. I'm scared!"

She spoke softly to him, and he listened. "Ed, never be afraid. No matter what, Ed, God is always with you. God loves you. You are fixed in God's memory." Then she was gone.

Ed opened his eyes. Karen was sitting at the end of the couch. She handed him a cup of freshly brewed coffee. He reached for it and told her about both dreams—the Cave of Troubles and the grizzly bear and his mother.

His wife listened in silence, then said with a smile, "I'm remembering now why your mother gave you your middle name, Emmanuel. God with us."

Ed smiled too. "What are we going to do, Karen?"

Again, she smiled. "I guess you had better look into that bundle on your right shoulder."

They did so together, and by the new year, they had a plan, a resolution, and a way to lighten the bundle on his left shoulder.

Resilience

The prompt posed to my writing group was "resilience." Ah, such an important psychological construct for humans. The prompter suggested some online links to various articles and discussions about resilience, which I examined for creative ideas. Those links led me to more until I followed a maze of professional literature through publications like *Psychology Today* and the offerings of numerous psychological websites.

I found research articles on developing resilience in children, resilience in teenagers, resilience among holocaust survivors and survivors of addiction, abuse and trauma of all types. I read and reread about resilience until my eyes were crossed and my mind was exploding with ideas. I wrung my hands in despair, watching the clock, counting the minutes until I had to share what I had written, and screamed, "What should I write?"

I calmed myself, finding my instinctual, resilient self. "Focus," I said. "Focus. What is the most important thing? What is the essence of resilience?"

I relaxed my shoulders and breathed deeply. After some minutes, I knew.

Resilience cannot happen without hope. In all of literature, the clients and research subjects could be resilient because somewhere in the depths of their souls, there was hope—even if that slice of hope was very thin, a mere glimmer, it was still there.

So, I offer this simple haiku that explains resilience:

Resilience is
A rope pulled upward by hope
Who cheers, "Yes, you can!"

Part 8: Welcome to Readers' Theater

Readers' Theater is another way to tell a story, employing a team approach to storytelling. The name includes a reference to reading because the participants read the script smoothly, flawlessly and expressively rather than memorizing lines. It is theater because the readers use theatrical techniques such as expression, facial and body language, voice changes, music and props to enhance the performance.

I always used Readers' Theater in the classroom as a strategy to build fluency in reading and encouraged my teacher education students to use it in their classrooms too.

Readers' Theater, however, is not just for children. Adults of all ages love it too. I belonged to an adult Readers' Theater group for a little over a year. The members of this group wrote their scripts, then performed them for various audiences.

The scripts and parodies included here address the themes of clutter and choice.

Clutter in the Gutter

CHARACTERS

PHYLLIS, SALLY and CINDY; three retired women who have been friends since college.

PHYLLIS'S APARTMENT.

PHYLLIS is downsizing when her two friends stop by for a visit. She is holding up an old wedding gown when there is knocking at the door.

PHYLLIS

Come in. Hi, Cindy. You brought Sally! I didn't think I'd see you today, Sally.

CINDY

I told Sally we had to rescue you today. You're officially in your fifth day of down-sizing. I figured if you lasted this long, I'd bring you a fifth of joyful juice!

SALLY

I heard her say fifth and jumped in the car.

(looking at the gown)

Is that your wedding dress? Thinking of a return performance?

PHYLLIS

You mean get married again? In this? A 2020 senior bride in a size eight polyester blend with embossed roses from the seventies? No thanks. Been there, done that. Didn't take, moved on!

SALLY

So what happens to it?

PHYLLIS

I offered it to a preschool teacher for her dress-up corner, but she refused it. Kids want to dress up in the Barbie and Ken style. Into the Goodwill box it goes. They can put it with their Halloween costumes next year. Just right for a Bride of Frankenstein!

SALLY

(looking around)

Wow, you've been busy. Look at all these boxes. And every one has a label. You sure are organized.

PHYLLIS

You know me—organized to a fault. And I did my research too. I read *The Art of Discarding*, *Goodbye Things*, *Clutter Intervention* and my favorite, *Downsizing for Dummies*.

CINDY

What did they say?

PHYLLIS

They all pretty much say the same thing. Pull up your big girl panties, get a grip, and get it done!

CINDY

I admire you. Did you find anything exciting in your clutter? Anything risqué?

PHYLLIS

Nope. Remember all the love letters on scented stationery I kept for all those years, even after you-know-who followed someone else's scent? I burned them in a campfire a year ago. I don't want my children to find any stuff they don't need to know about!

CINDY

I should do the same. Ronnie and I have some pretty erotic stuff from our younger years.

PHYLLIS

You'd better take care of it before your kids have to. Did I tell you what happened to Tim, the supervisor in my office?

SALLY

What happened?

PHYLLIS

He and his twin brother and their wives were the only ones left to clean out their grandparents' house. They spent days going through this farmhouse that their grandparents had lived in for almost sixty-five years. When they got to the final recesses of the attic, they uncovered a surprise.

CINDY

Surprise? What was it?

PHYLLIS

It was a very old machine. They didn't know what it was or how it worked. Then they found a box with other parts and printed instructions.

SALLY

So what was it?

PHYLLIS
A sex machine. A vintage sex machine!

CINDY
You're kidding!

SALLY
How did they know it was a sex machine?

PHYLLIS
The printed instructions!

SALLY
So, how does it work?

PHYLLIS
I don't know. We asked Tim to bring it in, but it was too large and heavy and awkward... and he was embarrassed. He said it was a small but pretty heavy square metal box with wires and a plug, and inside were... straps and attachments to put on... sensitive... parts of the body.

CINDY
You're kidding! What happens when it's turned on? Like, when the machine is turned on?

PHYLLIS
Vibrations! Vibrations come through the attachments, and the body parts they are attached to get all tickly and tingly... and then the couple, like, umm... hmm... Use your imagination!

SALLY
It sounds dangerous. I wonder if anyone ever got... like... maimed from using it.

PHYLLIS
I doubt it had the Good Housekeeping Seal of Approval.

CINDY
What did Tim think about his grandparents having a sex machine?

PHYLLIS
He said the four of them were so tired by the time they found it, they just started laughing. They laughed so hard they were crying and rolling on the floor! Then they tried to imagine their grandparents in... you know, various positions... and laughed even more!

SALLY
What did they do with it?

CINDY
Did they, you know, try it out?

PHYLLIS
Tim said he thought of that. He put on his most sexy face and said, "How about it, sweetie. Wanna give it a go?"

SALLY
Well?

PHYLLIS
He never saw the pillow that slammed into his head through the cloud of dust!

CINDY
Don't tell me they put it in the estate sale?

PHYLLIS
Oh, no. They knew all the neighbors would be coming, and they didn't want to have to explain what it was.

SALLY
Imagine holding an estate sale and needing a section for adults only!

CINDY
Maybe the historical society would want it. You know, put it in the local museum?

PHYLLIS
Tim's brother suggested that, and Tim did mention it to the president. She blushed and said the museum didn't have room.

SALLY
That's too bad. It is a historical item. If they advertised it, they'd get more visitors to the museum and more contributions.

PHYLLIS
The wives wanted to put it on *Antiques Roadshow*! The husbands just glared at them, giving a thumbs-down.

CINDY
There could be more sex machines in other attics and basements too. Who knows what apparatuses lie in the domiciles of a town's senior citizens!

SALLY
So where is it now?

PHYLLIS
Tim took it to the recycling center in town, to the section with old machinery and farm implements. He waited until he was all by himself, then discreetly added it to the pile. When he went back a week later, it was gone!

SALLY
It makes you wonder where it is...

CINDY
And if someone is trying it out...

PHYLLIS

Let's just say the first rule of cleaning out should be, get your clutter in the gutter before you flutter!

Live Tidy, Die Tidy

CHARACTERS

A mom and two adult daughters, JANEY and BECKY.

SETTING

MOM'S apartment. JANEY enters.

JANEY

Mom, what are all those boxes in the front yard? Our whole house is out there!

MOM

Good, Janey. You're here! Your sister is coming, and the two of you need to go through that stuff. The junkman is coming at two o'clock to take the leftovers to the dump.

JANEY

Junkman? Dump? What do you mean?

(looking around)

What has happened to all our stuff? Becky said something about you moving.

MOM

That's right, dear. I'm moving to a retirement village. I'll have a tiny condo and won't have room for much.

JANEY

Retirement village? What village? Where?

MOM

It's over in Centerville. It's called Tidy Retirement Village. Their motto is "Live tidy, die tidy." They limit the number of personal possessions a resident can have—one chair, one bed, one place setting, one appliance, one electronic device…

JANEY

Only one? What if you need more? What if I want to come for lunch? Do I have to bring my own dishes and a chair?

MOM

Either that or I can borrow dishes and chairs from the community closet. It's just what I wanted! A small place, easy to keep clean—and no clutter. The simple life.

JANEY

What do you mean? Everyone has clutter. We all collect stuff and keep it. Maybe we'll need it someday or... just want it. You're not taking anything, like pictures or knickknacks or things that are special to you?

MOM

Of course I am. I'm taking these three plastic totes. I've gone through all my stuff. One tote has my off-season clothes, and the other two have my most cherished possessions... pictures of you, your sister and my grandchildren, and special things I've picked up on my travels.

JANEY

You mean you got it all in these totes?

MOM

Yup, these are the things I want with me for the rest of my life! Besides, I am only allowed up to three totes. And I know I won't be collecting more because of the clutter collection clause.

JANEY

The clutter collection clause? What's that?

MOM

The contract has a clutter collection clause. It means I won't have any more than the stated possessions at the monthly inspections.

JANEY

Monthly inspections? They check to see how much you have?

MOM

That's right, dear. It's a good system. I won't collect clutter if I know I could be fined for having more than the contract allows. And when they come to inspect, the fumigation crew comes too and fumigates the condo. I'll never have to worry about germs again. The condo will always be clean!

JANEY

Fumigation? That's crazy, Mom. Are you sure you want to do this?

MOM

Yes, this is perfect for me. When you and Becky come to visit, you'll go through the fumigation chamber in the lobby and all the germs will be sprayed away!

JANEY

That sounds awful, Mom. This place sounds so sterile!

MOM

I like sterile. I've always had to clean to keep you girls from picking up germs. I don't want to have to clean anymore. And I've always hated clutter. It was your father who was the collector. He was always buying things, and if he couldn't decide which one to buy, he bought one of each! I'd be rich if he hadn't wasted so much money.

Look! Your sister just pulled up. You go out and the two of you get busy sorting through that junk. I'm making us some lunch.

MOM exits. JANEY meets her sister outside.

JANEY

Hi, Sis. Mom is going crazy. She's moving to this place called Die Tiny, Live Tiny—Tidy—Retirement Village. She can only take three totes of stuff, and they do inspections and have fines and fumigate, and we have to be fumigated. It's crazy! We've got to do something!

BECKY

(pointing to the junk on the sidewalk)

What's all this stuff?

JANEY

It's everything else! She says we have to sort through it and take what we want. The junkman is coming at two o'clock to take the rest away.

BECKY

(looking at the junk and pointing)

There's my soccer trophy. And my yearbook. My Barbie dolls—all of them!

JANEY

(pointing)

And my dance collection... my tutu... my ballerina shoes!

BECKY

Our whole lives are here, Janey!

JANEY

I know. Beck, we have to do something! She doesn't want to do this. She'll regret it. We can't let all of this go to the junkyard.

BECKY

Listen, let's take some stuff to our cars so she'll think we sorted through it. When the junk man comes, after she pays him, we'll pay him more to take it to my house. We'll put it in my garage.

JANEY

Good plan, Becky! Perfect, in fact. One day, she'll be glad we didn't get rid of it.

JANEY and BECKY exit. After a pause, MOM enters with her cell phone and makes a call.

MOM

Audrey! How's life in Santa Fe? I can hardly wait to get there. Mission accomplished! The plan worked. The house is clean. Putting the stuff on the lawn sure got their attention. They knew I was serious about the junkman coming. And he did, right at two o'clock, and loaded the stuff into his truck. I have a feeling it didn't get dropped off at the junkyard, though... After I paid him and went back into the house, I noticed they each gave him more money. I'll bet you anything that stuff is crammed into Becky's garage! Her husband, Bob, will be furious, and they'll have a big fight about it. Becky will smooth things over by having Janey get her stuff to take to her own place. Then Becky and Bob will have makeup sex, and she'll buy him a new golf club. Makeup sex is never enough anymore—you have to buy a gift to go with it. That's probably why there's so much clutter in the world, because makeup sex is never enough!

Anyway, the stuff is gone. They can deal with it—or in about twenty-five years, their kids can deal with it!

They were aghast at the idea of the Tidy Retirement Community. I'll call them tomorrow and tell them I changed my mind and got a motor home instead.

I'm picking it up early tomorrow morning. I'll be on the road by noon. How many days do you think it will take me to get to Santa Fe?

A Choice Life

CHARACTERS

PHYLLIS, CINDY, SALLY; close college friends, now in their seventies.

SETTING

Java Café Coffee Shop. PHYLLIS is sitting at café table; speaks to CINDY and SALLY as they enter.

PHYLLIS

Hello, friends. I was hoping you didn't get stuck in the morning traffic.

CINDY

The freeway was crowded, but not too bad. We're ready for coffee.

PHYLLIS

(taking a sip of coffee)

Mmm... good.

(smacking her lips)

This is a good choice.

CINDY

What is it?

PHYLLIS

A hot, skinny caramel macchiato with a shot of peppermint, a twist of cinnamon, and a sniff of nutmeg.

SALLY

Sounds complicated. How did you ever stumble upon that concoction?

PHYLLIS

It's a research project! I've spent months trying every possible combination of flavors, and this is my top choice. My barista knows how to make it just to my liking!

CINDY

I'd never have the patience to go through all of that. I have two choices—a mocha latte or chai cappuccino. I save my choices for the pastries. But maybe I'll have something different today.

(studying the drink menu)

Caramel sounds good... and cinnamon... Let's see... Foggy bottom... I love a dark roast with caramel... or maybe hazelnut... with cinnamon... Oh, oh, they have cardamom... and almond... Yes, with caramel and cinnamon. No, just caramel, no cinnamon. That's it... a foggy bottom with caramel, cardamom and almond... Should I add the hazelnut?

SALLY

Make up your mind, Cindy.

CINDY

Okay, I'm ready. I'm excited to discover what I'll end up ordering when I get to the counter!

PHYLLIS

What are you having, Sally?

SALLY

Regular coffee, black.

CINDY

Be adventurous, Sally. Go wild!

SALLY

Okay, I'll have a plain doughnut too.

PHYLLIS

(reading from the menu)

Here are the doughnut choices: blackberry, blueberry, cranberry, strawberry or lingonberry with nuts, walnuts, pecans or pistachios. Cream-filled doughnuts: vanilla, lemon, strawberry. Then there are chocolate doughnuts: chocolate chip, chocolate on chocolate, glazed and, last, unglazed. Do you still want plain, Sally?

SALLY

Yes'm. Regular black coffee and a plain doughnut. Simple is sophisticated!

CINDY

You order first, Sally. I need to practice. Let's see... Foggy bottom with... caramel and almond, a shot of cardamom and hazelnut... no whipped cream... Ah, maybe a splash of whipped cream.

CINDY and SALLY go to the counter. PHYLLIS continues to read from the menu.

PHYLLIS

Kiss of the Morning Latte—put a blend of chocolate and orange in your morning espresso to start the day with sunshine. Open Your Eyes Tea—a blend of spices to brighten up your day. Top of the Morning Muffin—with Bailey's Irish Cream. Stick to Your Ribs Oatmeal Scone—filled with homemade granola, dates, pecans and orange zest. Sinful Cinnamon—tickle your taste buds with cinnamon, chocolate bits, caramel, cashews, pistachios and... Yes, this is legal... A sprinkle of weed. Oh, my!

CINDY and SALLY return with drinks.

CINDY

I could come here every day for a year and order something new every time.

SALLY

I figure you just can't go wrong with black coffee and a plain doughnut.

PHYLLIS

Have either of you ever been to the Queen's Imperial Chinese Palace? Talk about choices. Their menu has seven pages, all in fine print!

SALLY

Mert and I go there sometimes. He won't even look at the menu. He closes his eyes, opens to a page, points and whatever his finger lands on, he orders. We've had some interesting meals there.

CINDY

Ronnie and I go there with my sister and her husband. The last time, Ronnie refused to let us open the menus. He said, "Give me a number from one to... like one hundred forty-seven." Whatever number we said, that's what we ordered. It was kind of a fun game. Except for the boiled squid and sautéed bok choy topped with kimchi.

PHYLLIS

That reminds me. Talk about having to make a choice quickly! It's those rotaries and roundabouts. I was on Cape Cod last month. There must be a law that requires every town to have a roundabout. I took one where there were so many route numbers and signs, I just kept going around until I read each of them. I expected a cop to pull me over. Can you get arrested for going around and around on a roundabout?

CINDY

It's a good thing we're retired. We have more time to make choices.

SALLY

My mother used to say, "You kids have two choices for supper—take it or leave it."

CINDY

That was the rule at my house too.

PHYLLIS

Remember when televisions had three channels? Now my cable company prides itself on offering something like 950 of them!

CINDY

It's funny, isn't it, the way our world has changed? And with all the choices we have, it doesn't seem that we're any better for it.

SALLY and PHYLLIS nod in agreement

PHYLLIS

Well, ladies, it's time for me to get to Zumba class. I love that we meet every Tuesday morning for coffee. See ya next week, girlfriends!

SALLY

See ya. Don't break anything.

CINDY

Next week, we'll go wild!

Parodies

All That Clutter (Tune: Alouette)

All that clutter, Lordy, all that clutter.
All that clutter makes me want to cry!
Should I give it to the kids?
Should I give it up for bids?
To the kids?
Up for bids?
Ooooohhhhh...
All that clutter, Lordy, all that clutter.
All that clutter makes me want to cry!

A Mountain of Clutter (Tune: On Top of Old Smokey)

A mountain of clutter, all covered with mold,
Took it all to a yard sale, but none of it sold.
Took it to my children and all of their kids,
But all of them vanished and from me they hid.
I took it to Goodwill and thought they'd be pleased.

But the layers of fine dust just made them all sneeze.
I had to dispose of it before the rent was due.
He said if it lingered, I'd have to skidoo.
So I drove to the country and bought an old barn.
I stuffed it all in there. It worked like a charm.
Now if you have clutter, don't worry your head.
Stuff it in an old barn and live there instead.

Give Me a Home (Tune: Home on the Range)

Oh, give me a home,
Where the clutter has grown
But only the basics will stay.
Where never is found
A heap or a mound
And the house is so tidy all day.
Home, safe in my home,
In the anti-junk, clutter-free zone.
Where stuff can be banned
With the flick of a hand,
But its memory
Will last all my days.

How Many Choices (Tune: Blowin' in the Wind)

How many choices
Must I decide,
Before my life is done?
How many times
Must I change my mind
Before I end my run?
How many plans

Must I make or drop
Before the race is won?
The answer, my friend,
Is blowing in the wind.
The answer is blowin' in the wind.

Choices (Tune: I Love Paris)

I make choices in the morning.
I make choices in the night.
I make choices in the winter,
When it drizzles.
I make choices in the summer,
When it sizzles.
I make choices every hour,
Every hour of the day.
I make choices,
My, oh my, so many choices.
It's how I work and play.

Dinner Choices (Tune: Tammy)

I know the waiter
Is wanting my choice.
Choices, choices...
What shall I choose?
Should I get chicken,
But beef sounds so good.
Choices, choices...
What shall I choose?
Should I choose the fish,
Baked or broiled,

As my main dish?
My heart starts to beat wildly.
It's like a big test.
Wish I knew what entrée
Would satisfy me best.
Choices, choices...
What shall I choose?

Thank you for reading *My Storied Life*.
If you've enjoyed reading this book, please leave a review on your favorite review site. It helps me reach more readers who enjoy a good story.

Acknowledgments

I learned storytelling by osmosis when, as a toddler, my mother nestled me on her lap and told me the story of "The Little Red Hen" every time I asked. I adored my father, who told funny stories and made people laugh. When I discovered that storytelling was a real thing, with professional organizations and folks all over the world telling stories in their own way, I knew I was home.

I owe a debt of gratitude to all the workshop leaders, keynote speakers, and featured tellers of the National Storytelling Network, Northeast Storytelling, Northlands and a myriad of storytelling guilds across the country who schooled me in the art of storytelling.

Specifically, I thank my late friend Sara Slayton who was a masterful storyteller and left this world far too early, my friend Dr. Michael Seliger who listens to my stories with an analytic mind and open heart, and Susanna Liller for insisting that I should share my stories that touch the heart.

Thank you to all who join with me in this art form that brings joy and understanding to listeners of all ages.

About the Author

Dr. Phyllis A. Blackstone is a storyteller extraordinaire. During a teaching career of over forty years, she taught first through seventh grades, served as a literary specialist and curriculum coordinator, and taught undergraduate and graduate students. Early on, she discovered that storytelling was her preferred way to teach people new things, no matter what their age.

In retirement, she enraptures her listeners, sharing wisdom and truth through folktales, personal stories, and creative narratives. Her audiences include children, families, adults and senior citizens in venues ranging from classroom settings to nursing homes. What started as a pandemic project, to write all the real and imagined stories she had created, resulted in this eclectic collection that will tickle the funny bone and bring a tear to the eye.

Phyllis is a member of the National Storytelling Network, Northeast Storytelling, and the Healing Story Alliance. She is also a founding member of three storytelling guilds: the Bluff Country Tale Spinners in La Crosse, Wisconsin, the Western Order of Dedicated Storytellers (WOODS) in Farmington, Maine, and the Brunswick Area Storytelling Society (BASS) in her hometown of Brunswick, Maine, where she currently resides.

She is the organizer of the Maine Storytelling Muster, the annual story swap for Maine storytellers, and fans of storytelling. She hosts monthly storytelling swaps at BASS and at Grampa's Garden and Coffee Bar in Brunswick.

In her spare time, Phyllis enjoys traveling, attending live theater performances, walking in the woods, and snowshoeing.

You can find information for Phyllis's upcoming performances at blackstonestoryteller.com.

If you're interested in having Phyllis speak to your group or organization about this book or to conduct a storytelling program, you can contact her at emeraldlakebooks.com/blackstone.

The Earl and Alice Blackstone Family

Back, left to right: Vernon, Earl (father), Alice (mother) Roger

Front, left to right: Phyllis, Barbara, Earlyne, Joyce, Ruth

Circa: 1955

For more great books, please visit us at
emeraldlakebooks.com.

Made in the USA
Middletown, DE
02 December 2021